Conservative Essays
For the Modern Era

By

Gregory E. Parker

Parker Press

A Book Publishing Company

DEDICATION

For my son Jean-Luc Christian Parker

A special thank you to my wife Tasha, my brother Chris, my sister LaShawn, my wonderful mother Lois, my father Willie, and my great friends Allen West, Christy Mowrey, Alfonzo Rachel, Eric, Kelly Burton, and others for believing in me.

CONTENTS

Foreword By Allen B. West

IT IS THE SEMINAL question that any parent must ask themselves: what shall I impart to my children? For some, it has everything to do with substantial wealth or possessions, material gain. Then there are those who never consider this question and prefer to have their progeny to remain in whatever state they found themselves. What we must come to realize is that the greatness of America has been about generations being committed to passing on a better America than what existed for them. It is that exact belief that enables me to be who I am and where I am today. My parents, Herman (Buck) Sr. and Elizabeth (Snooks) West made a choice to set the conditions for me to achieve greater than themselves.

I will never forget the day back in 1975 when my parents sat me down back in the historic Old Fourth Ward neighborhood of Atlanta at our home and gave me their challenge. They wanted me to be the first military officer in our Family. My Dad was a World War II Army Corporal. My older brother was a Vietnam War Marine Lance Corporal. They set the bar higher for me. Back in 2014, I had a book published that shared the story of how my folks raised me and inculcated strong, principled conservative values within me without my knowing. They laid a foundation that was integral in building the man I am to this day, and it is still being completed. My folks understood the words of Proverbs 22:6 (NASB): *"Train up a child in the way he should go. Even when he is old, he will not depart from it."*

I have to wonder, what would a book or collection of thoughts from my dad to me have looked like? I recall Mom and Dad imparting such wisdom to me like, *"a man must stand for something or else he will fall for anything," "a hit dog will holler," "the measure of a man is not how many times he is knocked down, but how many times he rises,"* or my favorite *"Son, never read your own press or drink your own tub water."*

I was raised in different times and days. Life seemed truly simple when we compare it to the challenges our children and grandchildren face today.

Today, I am a parent and a Dad to two daughters, Aubrey and Austen. Aubrey, our oldest, has set out on her own to attend Physician Assistant school, having completed her bachelor's and master's degrees. Our youngest, Austen, is an Army ROTC Cadet, a college junior seeking to be the fifth generation of military service member from our Family and the first female. I am constantly speaking to them about the world and trying to impart life lessons to them so that Proverbs 22:6 can resonate and be the defining theme of our relationship…as it was with my parents.

But what would it look like if I could put thoughts to paper and provide them a guidebook for this time?

Well, thanks to Gregory Parker, I do not have to endeavor to do such. Gregory, a friend I met a few years ago, was the first African-American and youngest to win an election as a County Commissioner in Comal County (Texas) history. Greg has penned this book "Conservative Essays for the Modern Era" to his Son, Jean-Luc. Gregory is sharing with his son the all-important understanding of what classical liberalism modern conservatism are in an era of progressive socialism. As well, Greg is tackling other major issues for his son, such as freedom, liberty, identity politics, free market capitalism, our Second Amendment, and the growing threat of militant Islamic fascism.

Gregory has not just written a book for his son; he has written one for my daughters and your children as well. He is arming them with objective truth so that they may be able to be educated and informed citizens, not mindless sheep or subjects. This book is more than necessary in these days and times because if we as parents do not take this responsibility, others will see it as theirs.

Truth is not relative; there are absolutes. It is time parents, such as my Mom and dad, and Gregory, reestablish themselves and be the leaders in their households. This book is needed and will be a must-read for generations to come.

Lieutenant Colonel Allen B. West (US Army, Retired)
Member, 112th US Congress

Why I Wrote This Book

INITIALLY, HISTORY WAS CARVED into stone. It was etched into walls and rock, withstanding the test of time. Lore, tradition, and culture were passed down from father to son, from elders to younger generations. It kept alive the truth and provided examples of how things were, in the hope that future generations could learn from mistakes and build upon the success. Myth should never be confused with this practice, as they exaggerate, change form, and are used to change what was into an unidentifiable lie. History, while unpleasant as it may be, is still history nonetheless. Today, history seems to be written in pencil, quickly erased, and then rewritten to suit the narrative or agenda of the day. This revisionist history is seen in the thrust to substitute historical civil war monuments with newer social justice warrior heroes that are shrouded in controversy, myth, and relativism. The myths of the more modern heroes are being taught as history and truth. Common sense, critical thinking, and understanding of facts are the inconvenient nuisance hampering the pursuit of the socialist collective agenda.

The digital canvas has replaced chisel and stone. The Internet has supplanted the cave walls as the depository of knowledge. These are the mediums holding the last vestiges of truth, and it is in this medium I write these essays for you, Jean-Luc Parker. Your generation is the future leaders, the thinkers, and the hope for what has, up to this point, been the single greatest civilization the earth has ever known. The purpose of these essays is to provide a foundation and some guidance for you and your generation.

History has always been fixed. However, more and more, our history has become stories, myths that change and bend to agendas rather than stand as a testimony of time. I have watched our political leaders, the academic elite, and a compliant media move in the shadows, rewriting the past to shape the future. Civil discourse and the dissemination of facts have given way to pandering to our lowest common denominator. Words like "tolerance" have their actual definition altered to mean the blanket acceptance of anything, no matter how unpalatable or dishonest. Those who challenge this dishonesty, invoke factual data, or display reason or critical thinking are mocked, humiliated, and silenced in the public square and on campuses. These tactics are merely tools to create and maintain an ignorant society.

Son, in the analysis that follows, you will find an honest look at the issues that will define your generation. These critical issues will shape what type of country you and your children will face. Being a passive observer or a docile American witness while the country and the world change around you will no longer be an option in your era. You can no longer allow the rise of the mass media, mass politics, and massive government that benefit a relatively small group to have considerable leverage in determining the course of a whole society. It will be all the more important to be armed with the information needed to fight the lies, historical distortions, and propaganda. While there are numerous issues you will face, all could not be explained in the confines of these essays. Therefore, I penned the first essay as the foundation or standard to which you can thoughtfully examine other issues not listed within the bounds of this book.

Son, old men like me will fade into history, so I thought it prudent that I leave you, your children, and your generation with a part of me while also pointing the way to the truth. Edmund Burke said, *"The only thing necessary for the triumph of evil is for good men to do nothing."*[1] Jean-Luc, these pages contain the truth, my effort to do something rather than do nothing. I will end with this quote from Thomas Jefferson, *"...whenever the people are well-informed, they can be trusted with their own government; that whenever things get so far wrong as to attract their notice, they may be relied on to set them to rights."*[2] There is a war upon us, a war against the truth, a battle for the hearts and minds of your generation. It is your time now, this is your cause now, to pick up the mantle of truth and knowledge and the courage to stand resolute in the face of ignorance.

Chapter 1

FREEDOM AND DEMOCRATIC SOCIALISM

JEAN-LUC, I WAS SPEAKING with a friend in the Spring of 2016. While the conversation that transpired was quite pleasant, he did inquire of me a far-reaching question: Is the concept of "democratic socialism" truly obtainable? Now, the truth be told, my first instinct was to respond by saying it is clearly not possible, but I thought it would be prudent to reflect on the question before a hasty answer.

In this essay, I will seek to examine the subject of democratic socialism. However, before I do, I believe it is essential to briefly discuss the concept of individual freedom as it relates to civil society. While I by no means claim to have all the answers to what freedom is, nor do I possess the remedy for the lack thereof, what follows is my humble understanding of the question asked and a brief examination of individual freedom's role within government. It is also worth noting that I use the terms freedom and individual freedom quite interchangeably within the context of this essay.

1

Gregory E. Parker

Freedom

"General freedom in this sense is nevertheless impossible, for the freedom of each would founder on the unlimited freedom, i.e., the lack of restraint, of all others."[3] ~ Fredrick Hayek.

Webster's Dictionary defines freedom as the absence of necessity, coercion, or constraint in choice or action. While this definition is that of a pure construct of individual freedom, I would argue that in civil society, true individual freedom, as defined above, is not possible. Adam Smith, a famed philosopher and economist, stated, *"Every man, as long as he does not violate the laws of justice, is left perfectly free to pursue his own interest his own way..."[4]* Further, Adam Ferguson, Scottish philosopher and historian, echoed Smith's statement, *"Liberty or Freedom is not, as the origin of the name may seem to imply, an exemption from all restraints, but rather the most effectual applications of every just restraint to all members of a free society whether they be magistrates or subjects."* As we can see, given Smith's caveat of *"not violating the laws of justice,"* and Ferguson's *"most effectual applications of every just restraint"* there is a level of coercion or constraint in choice or action on freedom. This precursor for true individual liberty is imperative, albeit demanded by most within civil society. This request from civil society, with respect to limiting individual freedom or accepting the coercion or constraint in choice, centers on safety or freedom from harm.

2

For example, while an individual would have the freedom to drive a vehicle, an individual would not, and some would argue, should not have the freedom to drive that vehicle while ignoring all traffic lights, as it may result in a severe vehicular accident-causing possible injuries or death. One could also use this analogy: while an individual would have the freedom to move their fist in any direction they desire, does that individual have the freedom to plant said fist into another person's face? In essence, should your freedom to do as you desire supersede another's freedom to be safe from harm?

> *"They put up with their servitude…because they found some good in it: the slave is relieved of concern for securing his daily bread, for the master is obliged to provide him with the necessities of life."[5] ~ Ludwig von Mises.*

It is very natural to want to protect oneself from harm. I believe that society has an innate desire to seek safety or being safe from harm, and that desire for safety (collective safety) will always lead to reduced individual freedom. Moreover, given an individual will always choose collective safety and security over freedom, that reduction in freedom will inevitably lead to a gradual, if not the immediate, realization of socialism, even in the freest societies. Ludwig von Mises, a prominent economist, noted in his book *"Liberalism,"* that those without freedom sought out the servitude or the lack of freedom because they found good in it. He went on to say that those without freedom were free from the concern of security. [6]

We see this clearly in our current welfare system, coincidentally called the social safety net. In most of the United States, recipients of welfare benefits are making the equivalent of, depending on the state, as much as $49,175 annually. That is more than the average pre-tax first-year wage for a teacher in 11 states, more than the starting wage for a secretary in 39 states, and even more take-home money than an entry-level computer programmer in the three most generous states.[7] These same recipients have demanded, and in some cases, have become physically violent to keep the government bondage of welfare, i.e., their economic security. As Ludwig said, *"the slave is relieved of concern for securing his daily bread, for the master is obliged to provide him with the necessities of life."*

Numerous other examples exist of how the desire for safety continually trumps the desire for individual, economic, or political freedoms. Consequently, if it were more prudent for recipients to work and find more security in their liberty, the recipients would act and choose to work. This was evidenced by the first settlers' arrival at Jamestown in 1607, setting up a common storehouse of grain from which colonists were supposed to take only what they needed and return what they could. Settlers owned no land of their own; all land was held in common and worked in common. The colonists quickly learned that no one is responsible for anything when everyone is entitled to everything. It became painfully clear that a colonist who started his work day early or stayed late received the same provision of food as a colonist who showed up late, went home early, or didn't work at all. After two years, the Jamestown colonists were reduced to eating shoelaces and rats. Captain John Smith took control of the colony, scrapped the socialist communal model, and granted each colonist a parcel of land. Smith instituted individual responsibility and freedom, thereby stabilizing Jamestown. Subsequently, the following winter, only 15 percent of the settlement's population died from disease and starvation compared to 60 percent the previous winter.[8]

Another example, in the first three months after the State of Maine required welfare recipients to work or volunteer at least 20 hours a week, caseloads of welfare recipients plummeted by nearly 80 percent, falling from 13,332 welfare recipients in December 2014 to 2,678 in March 2015.[9] Former welfare recipients, Maine business owners, and citizens expressed satisfaction with the results. *"For too long, our famous work ethic and individualism has been eroded by a destructive undercurrent of dependency and entitlement among too many of our able-bodied workforce."*[10]

As you can see, son, it is apparent from the evidence that this shifting of security for one's food and basic necessities from the government to the individual had noticeable positive effects. It is evident that an individual will always choose collective safety and security over freedom unless their own individual freedom best obtains that safety and security.

Political leaders are pushing victimization and promise safety from anything that makes one feel uneasy. This victimization has created a willful servitude or relinquishment of individual freedom for safety. It has led to an ever-growing distortion on freedom that is now pervasive in the modern era. Liberal government policies that hand out the privilege of economic or political security are nevertheless rapidly creating conditions in which the striving for such security tends to become stronger than the love of freedom.[11]

It should be noted that I am not advocating servitude of any kind or justifying the historical enslavement of any race. I am merely describing the context and construct of freedom as it exists today, thereby setting the stage for the remainder of this essay and the following chapters.

Arbitrators of Freedom

In a civil society, as noted above, citizens not only demand to limit their individual freedom for safety, but they also require an arbitration element be in place to contend with such individuals that use or abuse that personal liberty for harm. I would argue that the arbitration element in a civil society is that of the family and government, respectively. While it is evident the family unit is the first level of arbitrator of freedom, the government, unfortunately, takes over when the first is missing or unwilling to act, i.e., foster care or child protective services. We are by now all aware of the socially familiar principle that your mother should get control of you now, or the police will do it for her later.

Some would still argue this safe-from-harm concept, as noted above, is still coercion or constraint in choice. As absolute freedom, while wished for, would be complete anarchy and chaos, I believe this safe-from-harm concept is centered on conscious, concern, and consequences.

> *"If there is any function of government that all but the most extreme anarchist libertarians will agree is appropriate, it is to protect individuals in society from being coerced by other individuals, to keep you from being hit over the head by a random or nonrandom stranger."*[12] *~ Milton Friedman.*

Let me explain. An individual in civil society still has the freedom to plant their fist into another individual's face. However, I believe people suppress this desire, if you will, for committing this brutal act or acting on that personal liberty by one's conscience, a sense of right and wrong, one's concern for others' well-being, and the consequences for the use or abuse of that freedom. The first arbitrator, the family, is tasked with teaching and reinforcing these essential behavioral traits.

Conscious concern and consequences for using individual freedom are expected in a civil society. Family and government arbitrators are tasked with setting the consequences and constructing the justice system. It is worth noting that I believe the role of the government arbitrator within a civil society should remain minor but efficient and always err on the side of individual freedom. However, the family arbitrator should remain sizable regarding its influence and strong regarding its bond with the individual.

> *"Government is needed only to enforce these abstract rules, and thereby to protect the individual against coercion, or invasion of his free sphere, by others."*[13] ~ *Fredrick Hayek.*

Distortions on Freedom

> *"This country began with the pursuit of freedom, but the arbitrator of that freedom has become its captor."* ~*Gregory Parker.*

Fredrick Hayek, economist, and philosopher, noted that a government strong enough to protect individuals against violence from fellow citizens would abuse that power sooner or later to suppress the freedom they had previously secured to enforce their own presumably greater wisdom.[14] I call this "presumably greater wisdom," a distortion of freedom. We can see these complications and distortions arise as the government arbitrator, under the declaration of the public good, public safety, or collective security, wrongly pursues a strategy of equalizing individual freedoms through reduction or supplementation rather than just performing as an actual arbitration factor between the individuals and abusers of freedom. Using the before mentioned example, the government arbitrator, not merely content with arbitrating between the individual who used his freedom to drive a vehicle through all traffic lights, thus killing someone, would remove all freedom to use vehicles from every person, thereby pursuing a strategy of equalizing freedom by reduction. Conversely, the government arbitrator that provides all individuals with a vehicle and subsequently provides tolerances for that freedom to drive through all traffic lights is thereby pursuing equalizing freedoms by supplementation.

These distortions on freedom by reduction or supplementation exist and are noticeably evident within the second amendment debate raging in our modern age. While the details are left to another essay, I will attempt to surmise here. Opponents of the second amendment seek to reduce everyone's individual freedom by removing all firearms. Nevertheless, they fail to understand that the individual freedom for safety afforded by firearms outweighs the collective safety offered by the government. Furthermore, the government's continued failure in the arena of collective safety and security, both nationally and locally, only increases the push for individual freedom of protection through firearms.

Given the myriad of religious, economic, and environmental factors, the family arbitrator has significant latitude regarding this distortion effect on individual freedom. These factors, too numerous to delve into within the confines of this essay, play a large part in why a strong family is critical to preserving individual freedom as it is relevant to the government.

As mentioned above, a strong family arbitrator, critical to preserving individual freedom, is tasked with the instruction of conscious, concern, consequences, and the discipline to follow through. There are noticeable declines and changes in the family arbitrator core structure and the attitude toward achieving the before mentioned task. We see this clearly in the black community.

Instilling discipline of the children within the family has traditionally been the role of the father. The father is notably absent from the black family. Black children stand in contrast to any other racial group, with an astonishing 64 percent of black children growing up with only their mother as of 2014.[15] In contrast, in 1865 or prior, when black marriages were in some cases illegal, 63.5 percent of black children were growing up with both parents in the home.[16] I believe this erosion of the black family has given rise to a lack of consciousness, concern, and consequences being taught in the home. Accordingly, black children are twenty times more likely to go to prison, and FBI data concluded that 4,906 black people were murdered by blacks from 2010 to 2011. That aggregates to more blacks killed at the hands of other blacks in two years than were lynched in all the years from 1882 to 1968 under Jim Crow.[17]

This demise of the black family has not been missed over time. Gunnar Myrdal, a Swedish Nobel Laureate economist, sociologist, and politician, noted in his 1944 research on black America that black family life was, in his words, *"disorganized."* Their sexual morals were lax, and they were prone to aggression and violence.[18] Myrdal noted that low standards of efficiency, low reliability, and low ambition were displayed in the black community.[19]

While I just briefly used the black family as an example, the disappearance of discipline within the family arbitrator without respect to race has given apparent rise to the departure of conscious, concern, and consequences being taught in the modern home. The modern-era concept of "Gentle Parenting," where discipline and the word "No" are not used, is, in my mind, another factor in the demise of instruction of conscious, concern, and consequences. Further, according to John Rosemond, author and family psychologist, if parents effectively keep absent the word "No" from the home and tolerate the child's whining, demanding, and manipulation, it will most certainly lead the child to a mistaken belief that something can be gained for nothing. Not only is this false, but it is also one of the most dangerous, destructive attitudes a person can acquire. He also noted that these perverse actions by parents might explain why the psychological health of children in the 1950s was considerably better than the psychological health of today's children.[20]

> *"Children who grow up believing in the something-for-nothing fairy tale are likely to become emotionally stunted, self-centered adults."*[21] *~ John Rosemond.*

I believe the difficulty with this concept of gentle parenting is that it allows children to exercise individual freedom

without restraint, which, as noted above, is quite problematic.
Doctor Leonard Sax, family physician, psychologist, and
author of *"The Collapse of Parenting: How We Hurt our Kids
when We Treat Them Like Grown-Ups,"* noted that most
American parents are confused and are in the wrong
direction. He further pointed out that some parenting experts
have instructed adults to offer their children choices rather
than giving commands to the children, and parents have
taken this false advice to heart. This false advice has produced
a situation where the hierarchy of parent above child no
longer exists. Instead of parents exercising their authority,
they focus on making children happy and boosting their self-
esteem rather than discipline.[22] This parenting style only
pushes the burden of teaching consciousness, concern, and
consequences on the government arbitrator. One can surmise
this creates adults who are only concerned with and/or feel
for themselves. These adults have little, if any, consequences
for their actions. This, in turn, reduces the individual freedom
this practice claims to want to promote.

All these factors and failures are causing the government
arbitrator to now intervene, expanding their role
exponentially, thereby creating ever-larger distortions on
individual freedom. These government-created distortions on
freedom become increasingly demanded by civil society to
counterbalance the failures of the family arbitrator. We have
seen this in modern times with the increasing use of metal
detectors and police officers in schools to counterbalance the
disciplinary failures of the family arbitrator. We now see

schools deciding to clarify the line between the family and the government arbitrator. A Catholic High School for Boys in Little Rock, Arkansas, is teaching its students personal responsibility by not allowing students' parents to drop off students' forgotten lunches.[23] A Portuguese school chose to post a message to all parents that reads:

> *"Dear parents*
> *We would like to remind you that magic words such as hello, please, you're welcome, I'm sorry, and thank you all begin to be learned at home. It's also at home that children learn to be honest, to be on time, diligent, show friends their sympathy, as well as show utmost respect for their elders and all teachers. Home is where they learn to be clean, not talk with their mouths full, and how/where to properly dispose of garbage. Home is also where they learn to be organized, to take good care of their belongings, and that it's not ok to touch others. Here at school, on the other hand, we teach language, math, history, geography, physics, sciences, and physical education. We only reinforce the education that children receive at home from their parents."*[24]

As noted above with the second amendment debate, distortions on freedom by reduction or supplementation can and do undoubtedly appear in all policy issues. The New York City District Attorney, in April 2017, instituted a policy to allow illegal immigrants to plea to lesser crimes to avoid deportation. As a result, American citizens committing the same offense will face harsher punishment, given they are citizens.[25] As we can see, such distortions by the government arbitrator become increasingly convoluted and perpetual as the arbitrator pursues these strategies of equalizing freedoms for only one category of individuals. Inevitably, this leads to a complete erosion of freedom and an incorrect understanding of true individual freedom.

Conversations About Freedom

Invariably, any talk of freedom will unleash dual sides of the debate. Advocates for chaos will quote Benjamin Franklin's famous words, *"Those who would give up essential Liberty to purchase a little temporary safety deserve neither liberty nor safety,"* in a cry for anarchy.[26] Not many individuals who quote these words have any idea of their factual origin or what Franklin was saying when he wrote them.

Benjamin Franklin's words initially appeared in a letter he wrote in 1755 on behalf of the Pennsylvania Assembly to the Pennsylvania Governor. Franklin did not write this letter in an effort to warn about ceding his liberty to the government but as a legislator being asked to renounce his power to tax lands under his jurisdiction. The *"essential liberty"* to which Franklin referred is the right of the governance to tax to pay for collective security. Further, the *"purchase [of] a little temporary safety,"* Franklin complains, was not the ceding of power to a government in exchange for some promise of protection from external threat.[27] It referred to the governor, who wanted the legislature and Franklin to appropriate money for frontier defense (collective security) but did not want them to tax his friend's land to do so. The governor's friend later offered cash to fund the defense of the frontier with the provision that the legislature renounce its taxing authority over his land. Franklin was, therefore, facing a choice between making funds available for the collective defense or maintaining the legislature's right to tax.[28]

Proponents of more government control will use civil society's acceptance of the limits on its freedom for collective safety as an excuse to restrict that freedom further. Sen. Chuck Schumer (D-N.Y.) sought to justify this point of view in a 2012 Washington Post op-ed: *"No individual right is absolute, after all. While the First Amendment protects freedom of speech, no one has a right to falsely shout "Fire!" in a crowded theater..."* Justice Holmes' quote has mistakenly developed into a crutch for every politician or activist wanting the government arbitrator to have an ever-expanding role in the relinquishing of individual freedom. However, the quote is wildly misunderstood.

The actual quote from Justice Holmes in Schenck v. United States is, *"The most stringent protection of free speech would not protect a man in falsely shouting fire in a theater and causing a panic."*[29] Schenck v. United States had little to do with fires or theaters. The Court was deciding whether Charles Schenck, who coincidentally was the Secretary of the Socialist Party of America, could be convicted under the Espionage Act for writing and distributing a pamphlet.[30] The crowded theater remark was an analogy Justice Holmes wrote about the First Amendment not being absolute in his dictum or justice's ancillary opinion that didn't directly involve the facts of the case.

The two essential points of this quote are *"falsely shouting"* and *"causing a panic."* Shouting fire in a crowded theater is not necessarily a bad thing. If an actual fire were in progress, one would want an individual to use their freedom to yell fire. Further, in a theater containing very few patrons, such a declaration of fire would amount to a hollow utterance. The key is falsely shouting and causing panic. Moreover, one could still conceivably use their freedom to shout fire in a crowded theater, and the arbitrator must understand and deal with the consequences of such freedom.

Proponents of more government control want to extend that collective safety now to include speech that may hurt individual feelings. Consequently, individual freedom of speech has devolved into a battle over feelings rather than freedom. Advocates, using this collective ideology, claim that 'hate speech' or merely any speech that does not fit into their narrow agenda should be banned by the government. They have even taken to reporting speech they disagree with to the police. Moreover, proponents of more government control have begun to violently assault people as a means to terrorize and protest speakers; supporters have deemed to incite hate. This violence is not only dangerous but frighteningly reminiscent of socialist governments cracking down on dissenting ideas and clearly undermining their entire argument while exposing their deceit.

As we conclude this brief look at freedom, we now have
the foundation for moving forward with the rest of this essay
and future essays. I accept as accurate the failures of the
family arbitrator and that the distortions by the government
arbitrator have become increasingly convoluted and
produced an endless pursuit of equal freedom for a certain
few and not true freedom for all. These distortions construct
the perfect incubator for a political and economic move
toward socialism, which will erode our freedom.

> *"A major problem in achieving and preserving a free society is
> precisely how to assure that coercive powers granted to
> government in order to preserve freedom are limited to that
> function and are kept from becoming a threat to freedom."*[31]
> ~ Milton Friedman.

Adam Smith, economist, and philosopher, knew the
concentration of government power as a great danger to civil
society and protection from a tyrannical government to be a
perpetual need. That is why I hold fast to the notion that we
as a society must always fight for freedom. Fight with ideas,
with words, and sometimes with guns. I say these words not
to scare or offend but to provoke those who stand for
freedom. I believe that a society's overwhelming desire to be
safe and the inherent tendency of government to recognize no
restraints on its operation or collective intent will
undoubtedly and continually push even the freest societies
toward socialism.

Gregory E. Parker

Democratic Socialism

Now that we have considered freedom in the context of civil society and government, we can now focus our attention on the concept of democratic socialism. Based on the common societal understanding, one would consider the two individual political and economic freedoms to be exclusive to one another. Moreover, that same societal common knowledge would have one believe that neither could exist within the same economic or political systems. In so much as there would be no incentive for party bosses or tyrants who run these socialist societies to allow for democracy. In essence, why would a socialist leader want to allow any democratic outcome to an election that could topple his grip on power? Why would a socialist leader want free speech where ideas other than state propaganda could be heard?

We can see from Alexis de Tocqueville that democracy, under its common societal understanding of a 'free society,' or in the context of individual freedom, could not exist in a socialist society. Democracy broadens the sphere of personal liberty, while socialism restricts it. Democracy attaches all possible value to each man, while socialism makes each man a mere number. "*Democracy and socialism have nothing in common but one word: equality. Democracy seeks equality in liberty, while socialism seeks equality in restraint and servitude.*"[32]

With that said, we would need to define democratic socialism at its core outside its standard societal definition to obtain a clearer understanding of not only the existence of

18

socialism in the United States but also its citizens willingly adopting socialism by democratic vote.

What is Democratic Socialism?

Confucius once said, *"When words lose their meaning, people will lose their liberty."* I would add to that profound statement, *"When society changes words, people lose their liberty."* In today's modern age, there are several definitions of democratic socialism, depending on whom you speak to. Therefore, I believe the best explanation would emerge from an admitted socialist's own words.

> *"I think it [Democratic Socialism] means the government has got to play a very important role in making sure that as a right of citizenship, all of our people have health care; that as a right, all of our kids, regardless of income, have quality child care, are able to go to college without going deeply into debt; that it means we do not allow large corporations and moneyed interests to destroy our environment; that we create a government in which it is not dominated by big money interest. I mean, to me, it means democracy, frankly."*[33] ~ Bernie Sanders.

The term democratic socialism is not new. A few decades ago, "social democracy" was the word of choice for socialists. Social democracy, according to Webster's dictionary, is a political movement that uses principles of democracy to change a capitalist country to a socialist one or a country that uses both capitalist and socialist practices. Considering

Bernie Sanders's comments on the definition of democratic socialism, it appears a socialist system by democratic means is precisely what he seeks.

We can also see, from his comment above, that the word democracy is important here because I believe the use of the word overpowers in his remarks. Not only does he use the word democracy, but also *"right of citizenship"* or *"a right to,"* providing the comment a sense of fairness and equality. However, the use of the word democracy and its overarching sentiment in his comment is misleading to imply a sense of individual freedom and fairness while attempting to conceal a collective societal agenda. We can distinctly comprehend this by his choice of words: *"government has got to play a very important role in making sure,"* followed by a list of items to construct as rights of the people, creating a more significant role for the government arbitrator, which will create more massive distortions on individual freedom. In essence, he is pursuing a socialist system by democratic means.

Although history provides clear examples where socialism has typically been imposed at the point of a gun rather than as a result of free and fair elections, there is no real problem in the US with achieving such a socialist system democratically. However, the democratic process surrounding individual, political, and economic freedoms provides socialist beliefs the precise foothold needed to continue to pursue the very reduction of those freedoms. Socialists generally exploit this democratic process, claiming to fight for more freedom or equality, as in the case of Sanders's comment. That claim for new freedom and equality is nothing more than the old claim for creating equality through the redistribution of wealth. Ultimately, that same democratic process will be denied to others and their struggles. Consequently, democratic socialism exposes its own deceit.

In the term, "democratic socialism" democratic the adjective or word that adds to, and socialism is the noun or object that is at its root. Socialism is a fashionable buzzword in today's society. Researchers for the Journal of Democracy found that fewer than 50 percent of Americans thought democracy was necessary. This sharply contrasts with older generations, of which 75 percent said voting in free and fair elections was essential.[34] A recent survey found that 43 percent of millennial respondents under 30 had a favorable view of socialism.[35] However, a CBS/New York Times survey found that only 16 percent of millennials could accurately define socialism, while 30 percent of Americans over 30 could.[36] Consequently, even more disturbing, a Reason-Rupe survey found that those ages 18-24 supporting socialism did not favor government-running businesses, and when asked whether they want the government or private markets leading the economy, they chose private markets 2 to 1 (64 percent versus 32 percent).[37] There is undoubtedly a detachment from millennials and their view of socialism.

It is worth noting that as I move throughout this essay, I consider communism and socialism to be synonymous in terminology. Marx and Engels, the fathers of modern socialism, also applied these terms without distinction.

Moreover, most modern-era socialists and communists acknowledge there is no distinction.[38] Hitler himself declared in one of his public speeches, National Socialism and Marxism are the same."[39] Hitler further stated he was an enemy of capitalism. Communism is socialism practiced at a high level.

> "We are socialists; we are enemies of today's capitalistic economic system for the exploitation of the economically weak, with its unfair salaries, with its unseemly evaluation of a human being according to wealth and property instead of responsibility and performance, and we are all determined to destroy this system under all conditions."[40]

Socialism is an economic and political arrangement based on public or collective ownership of production. Socialism places emphasis on equality rather than any notable attainment and values workers by the total amount of time they put in rather than by the amount of value they produce. Capitalism, which I will examine in more depth in another essay, is grounded on private property rights, profit and loss, and a price system, whereas socialism is constructed on bureaucratic central planning and collective ownership. Advocates of socialism believe that it creates equality and provides economic security. We can understand this equality argument in our modern age given the tremendous engagement for political equality for transgender people, economic security with the income wage gap, and any number of other so-called trendy causes today. Conversely, this socialist equality to be achieved and maintained by democratic means seems to belong to the world of utopias.[41]

History suggests that economic freedom is necessary for political freedom; it is not the only condition. Several countries worldwide, such as Spain, Germany, and the United Kingdom, all practice some level of socialism or a lack of economic and political freedom. Milton Friedman noted in his book *"Capitalism and Freedom"* that it is possible to have economic arrangements of capitalism and political arrangements that limit society's freedom together.[42] Economists call this socialized sectors or mixed economies.

A mixed economy is an economic structure that features characteristics of both capitalism and socialism. This mixed economy allows a level of private economic freedom and allows governments to impede economic activities to achieve social aims. Governments are involved in planning the use of resources and can exercise control over the private sector. Governments could seek to redistribute wealth by taxing the private sector and using tax revenue to promote social objectives. China, while under the control of the Communist Party, introduced a series of reforms that brought back elements of a capitalist system.

Margaret Thatcher, former Prime Minister of England, brought capitalist reforms back to her country as the Labour Party had put the British economy well on the path to socialism. Thatcher understood the allure of socialism but recognized the fundamental flaws and pitfalls.

"Only two political philosophies, only two ways of governing a country. One is the Socialist-Marxist way in which what matters is not the people but the State. In which decisions affecting people's lives are taken from them instead of being taken by them. In which property and savings are taken from the people instead of being more widely held among them. In which directives replace incentives. In which the State is the master of the individual, instead of the servant. The other, is a free economic system which not only guarantees the freedom of each individual citizen, it is the surest way to increase the prosperity of the nation as a whole."[43]
~Margaret Thatcher.

Given the levels of individual economic or political freedom people are willing to give up, as noted earlier in this essay, it is reasonable to assume that there are levels of socialism, economic, or political limitations people are unwilling to tolerate. Therefore, I consider democratic socialism to be the continued pursuit of reducing individual economic and political freedoms by democratic vote. While some may seek such coexistence, it is clear that socialism reduces individual, economic, and political freedoms, thereby making it irreconcilable and continuously in conflict with democracy. And that conflict, as Mises explained, is a fight to protect the masses from the status of poor slaves entirely at the mercy of irresponsible dictators.[44]

Characteristics of Socialism

Socialism has three distinct main characteristics. These characteristics of socialist thought are not confined to any one economic status, political party, or even country. Ludwig noted that even opponents of socialism support socialist ideas.[45] Milton Friedman also found that leaders in capitalist countries cheer the collapse of socialism in other nations yet continue to favor socialist solutions. In his research, he found that governments of so-called capitalist countries are just as inept as governments of communist countries in dismantling any of their socialist practices.[46] Unfortunately, the US is no exception to socialist influence, as we shall see.

One of the critical characteristics of socialism is centralized or **collective ownership** of production. Karl Marx, in his book *"The Communist Manifesto,"* considered the individual to be highly inefficient and the community to be the most efficient means of economic production. He and other socialist leaders of their time regarded freedom of thought and private ownership as the root evil of nineteenth-century society.[47] In the modern era, as before, socialists disdain private property, private enterprise, and the profit motive. They believe such actions to be robbery, and the instruments of production should be owned by the people and operated for the people, i.e., the public. Under socialism, public ownership can assume the form of nationalization of private enterprises, municipal or regional enterprises, or cooperative enterprises.

In this modern era, the government does not need to own or nationalize stores or factories to direct production. The current over-regulatory environment in America acts as a substitute for direct government ownership of production.

Socialism fails in so much as when everyone owns something, no one owns it, and no one has a direct interest in maintaining or improving its condition.[48] Private property and private ownership in general and as the means of production are the bedrock of individual, political, and economic freedom. Such ownership is the outward display of freedom and individual thought and action. To be secure in one's person and property dates back throughout history. For this reason, socialists want to destroy this superior purpose of freedom.

> *"Private property creates for the individual a sphere in which he is free of the state. It sets limits to the operation of the authoritarian will. It allows other forces to arise side by side with and in opposition to political power. It thus becomes the basis of all those activities that are free from violent interference on the part of the state. It is the soil in which the seeds of freedom are nurtured and in which the autonomy of the individual and ultimately all intellectual and material progress are rooted." [49] ~Ludwig von Mises.*

Another essential characteristic of socialism is *Central Planning*. Socialists seek to plan and control economic activity through the central government. Central planning of the economy becomes necessary when collective or public ownership of production is established. The government will need to set production goals, wages, and the costs of goods and services for all areas of the economy. Such planning under socialism can lead to inefficient uses of production and other resources. No government agency could ever hope to plan and control all economic activity and prices on thousands upon thousands of products and transactions. This planning eventually leads to inefficient resource use, leading to longer wait times for items, an outright shortage of products, and the stifling of technological innovation. The United States sets production goals, wages, and the costs of goods and services using minimum wage laws, over-burdensome environmental and worker safety rules, and some degree of government involvement in the major sectors of the economy.

Socialists want to plan not only the economy but also individual lives. According to the Democratic Socialists of America, their long-term goal is to eliminate all but the most enjoyable work.

> *"Although a long-term goal of socialism is to eliminate all but the most enjoyable kinds of labor, we recognize that unappealing jobs will long remain."*[50] ~ *Democratic Socialists of America.*

Upon reading this, the first question should be, who will determine what is "enjoyable work." Each individual should have the freedom to decide what work is enjoyable. Now, the government will determine which jobs are enjoyable, socially fulfilling, or serve the greater good of the collective whole. Overburdensome regulations can be used to further some degree of government involvement in determining which jobs are socially fulfilling. The city of Chicago has now required students wanting to graduate high school to provide an acceptance letter from a city-approved four-year college, community college, branch of the armed services, or a trade school.[51] Diplomas will no longer be awarded to students seeking individual freedom to work in the family business or move to other countries after graduation. Chicago Mayor Rahm Emanuel stated, *"Starting with the freshman class, right now in high school in Chicago, ... if you graduate, you'll have to have a letter of acceptance from a college, a letter of acceptance from a community college or a letter of acceptance from the armed services or a letter of acceptance from a trade, carpenter or electrician."*[52] It is also noteworthy that each of the government options made available to students thrust those same students further under government control, even after reaching adulthood. It is an illusion to believe that such a system of planned socialism could be operated without losing individual freedom. Democracy and individual freedom are inextricably linked with capitalism and cannot exist where there is socialistic planning.

Another essential characteristic of socialism is *Egalitarianism*. Given that socialism is a reaction against capitalism's so-called injustice and miseries. Its proponents seek greater equality economically and politically. Socialism emphasizes the principles of freedom and equality while offering collectivism and servitude. As noted earlier in this essay, the continued fight for equality creates distortions on individual liberty. This concept of social equality creates a collective measurement to achieve fairness. Who is to decide what is fair? This notion of fairness is built on a corrupt idea, and every attempt to make the outcome fair for one or all inevitably creates unfairness for another or all. Thomas Sowell stated, *"Equality before the law is a fundamental value in a decent society. But equality of treatment in no way guarantees equality of outcomes. On the contrary, equality of treatment makes equality of outcomes unlikely since virtually nobody is equal to somebody else in the whole range of skills and capabilities required in real life. When it comes to performance, the same man may not even be equal to himself on different days, much less at different periods of his life."*[53] This flawed search for equality becomes a never-ending cycle that creates low standards and low expectations.

These characteristics assist in the understanding that all modern governments engage in some level of socialism. As stated in this essay, Ludwig surmised that even opponents of socialism support socialist ideas.[54] Today's international leaders and socialists believe President Obama opened the window for socialism to take root in America. I contend that President Obama only built upon the already thriving socialism in America. One need only look at the current public education system, the VA healthcare system, and the social security system to see that the United States is not only practicing socialism, it has opponents of socialism singing the praises of these programs.

Today, the Democratic Socialists of America boast some 70 members of the United States Congress, and even a presidential candidate claimed the mantle of a Democratic Socialist. I don't know which is more discouraging: that young people are becoming comfortable with socialism or that they have no idea what it is.

Venezuela and Socialism

"Socialism, in general, has a record of failure so blatant that only an intellectual could ignore or evade it." ~ Thomas Sowell

Socialists persist in the mistaken belief that socialism can work if only the right people are in charge or if it is properly implemented. They choose to conveniently forget the more than a century of failures and documented examples of the catastrophic damage socialism has had on countries such as Greece, France, the Soviet Union, and Brazil and their people. Notwithstanding, there is no more significant albeit classic example of the failures of socialism in modern memory than Venezuela.

Hugo Chávez was elected president in 1998 on a wave of democratic socialist support. He immediately passed a new constitution that consolidated his power, cracked down on dissent, jailed political opponents, and frayed the country's economy with a series of ill-planned economic overhauls. Between 1999 and 2016, the average per capita income in Venezuela rose by only 2 percent, while in the rest of Latin America and the Caribbean, the average per capita income increased by 41 percent.[55] Moreover, at the time of this essay, Venezuela, one of the most oil-rich nations in the world, has a 2,068 percent inflation rate. People are rummaging through trash cans because store shelves sit empty, and riots are commonplace. The situation has gotten so horrific that even the pro-socialist New York Times newspaper has taken note: *"Dying Infants and No Medicine: Inside Venezuela's failing Hospitals."*[56]

> *"The economic crisis in this country has exploded into a public health emergency, claiming the lives of untold numbers of Venezuelans. It is just part of a larger unraveling here that has become so severe it has prompted President Nicolás Maduro to impose a state of emergency and has raised fears of a government collapse. Hospital wards have become crucibles where the forces tearing Venezuela apart have converged. Gloves and soap have vanished from some hospitals. Often, cancer medicines are found only on the black market. There is so little electricity that the government works only two days a week to save what energy is left."*[57]

Again, in another article entitled *"Venezuela Drifts into New Territory: Hunger, Blackouts, and Government Shutdown,"* the New York Times stated the grim reality facing the country:

> *"The courts? Closed most days. The bureau to start a business? Same thing. The public defender's office? That's been converted into a food bank for government employees. Step by step, Venezuela has been shutting down. ... Venezuela keeps drifting further into uncharted territory. ... that is only the start of the country's woes. Electricity and water are being rationed, and huge areas of the country have spent months with little of either. ... the Mexican company that bottles Coke in the country has even said it was halting production of sugary soft drinks because it was running out of sugar."*[58]

The British Broadcasting Channel (BBC), also known for supporting the pro-socialist agenda, was equally puzzled by Venezuela's demise, as shown by their article entitled *"What has gone wrong in Venezuela?"* The Washington Post appears to have come to grips with the demise of the once strong nation in their editorial entitled *"Prepare for the worst: Venezuela is heading toward complete disaster,"* saying:

> *"Venezuela already suffers from the world's highest inflation rate — expected to rise from 275 percent to 720 percent this year — one of its higher murder rates and pervasive shortages of consumer goods, ranging from car parts to toilet paper. Power outages and the lack of raw materials are forcing surviving factories and shops to close or limit opening hours. According to a local survey cited by the Economist, the poverty rate is 76 percent, compared with 55 percent when Hugo Chávez, the late founder of the regime, took power in 1999."*[59]

Venezuela is home to the world's largest oil reserves, yet it has run out of gasoline. According to the newspaper El Nacional, one-third of Venezuela's 24 states – Miranda, Aragua, Lara, Barinas, Anzoátegui, Nueva Esparta, Bolívar, and Monagas, reported significant shortages in gasoline for sale in stations throughout these cities.[60] A Reuters investigation revealed that the current Venezuelan president's policy of exporting, often for very little or no profit, to countries who support Venezuela's socialist government has caused the 77 refineries to shut down.[61]

"Hundreds of Venezuelans found themselves stranded this week as the nation's gasoline supply ran out at stations throughout the nation's urban centers."[62]

In previous years, American leaders noted economists and Hollywood elite sang the praises of Hugo Chávez and his socialist policies. In 2009, President Obama said he "has a lot to learn" from Hugo Chavez, the former president of Venezuela. Nobel Prize-winning economist and Hillary Clinton economic advisor Joseph Stiglitz praised Hugo Chávez for his 'positive policies' during a visit to Venezuela.[63] Additionally, several actors, from Jamie Foxx and Danny Glover to Sean Penn, have visited Venezuela over the years. Sean Penn even claimed that Hugo Chavez was one of history's greatest leaders, and he called George Washington a 'loser' by comparison. *"I think he [Hugo Chávez] might be one of the best leaders of all time,"* Penn affirmed.[64] Of course, now, after Venezuela's collapse, we are hearing 'crickets' from American leaders, noted economists, and the Hollywood elite.

Now, the question must be asked: how did Venezuela get to this point? Some believe Hugo Chavez left the nation vulnerable economically by nationalizing energy assets while oil prices were high and spending the proceeds on widespread social programs. Economist Ricardo Hausmann outlined, due to current oil prices, Venezuela, as of 2015, will earn less than $18 billion this year from exports, while its payments on its $120 billion debt are $10 billion, leaving only $8 billion to import $37 billion of needed food and other

goods.[65] New York Times reporters Nicholas
Casey and Patricia Torres echoed Hausmann's conclusion
about Venezuela's dire situation, *"The growing economic crisis
(was) fueled by low prices for oil, the country's main export; a
drought that has crippled Venezuela's ability to generate
hydroelectric power; and a long decline in manufacturing and
agricultural production."*[66] Only those ignorant of economics
point to this explanation as the only actual cause of
Venezuela's failure, missing, of course, the apparent socialist
underpinning.

I assert that the combination of low oil prices, crushing
debt, and socialistic policies such as price controls contributed
to Venezuela's socialist failure. Mostly, the socialistic policies
that gave rise to the crushing debt and lack of strategic
forethought to anticipate lower oil prices may someday
reoccur.

While I will go into further detail on price controls in a
future essay, it is vital to note price controls are typically a
political response to economic price changes. Price controls
are often enacted to keep prices low and gain some measure
of political clout. To this day, price controls are a significant
undoing for Venezuela. Hugo Chavez introduced these price
controls on essential goods such as sugar, coffee, rice, milk,
and flour, to name a few. This was done to make essential
goods affordable to the masses, a policy continued under the
current Venezuelan president. These fixed prices led
businesses to complain that the new price control rules were
forcing them to produce these goods at a loss. Subsequently,

businesses could not or refused to produce the goods for government-run stores or shut down altogether.

With businesses unwilling to produce products because of price controls, a shortage of goods was immediately seen with long wait lines for what few products remained. Hoarding by citizens occurred, as well as black markets and cartel activities began to grip the economy, making it almost impossible to obtain the products. Thereby hurting the very citizens; the price controls were instituted to protect.

Moreover, price controls quickly become a power for the government to turn citizens against one another. Ralph R. Reiland reported in his 2007 Capitalism Magazine article on the Zimbabwean economic crisis that the price controls initiated by the Zimbabwean government only worsened the situation. To keep citizens in line, Zimbabwe's security forces were given the authority to observe citizens' e-mails and tap their phones. Business owners were threatened with jail and the nationalization of their companies if they did not obey pricing laws. These actions affected the incomes of Zimbabwean citizens. While Africa's income per person rose by 48 percent, in Zimbabwe, income per person declined by 25 percent.[67]

"Bread, sugar, and cornmeal, staples of every Zimbabwean's diet, have vanished, seized by mobs who denuded stores like locusts in wheat fields. Meat is virtually nonexistent, even for members of the middle class who have money to buy it on the black market. Gasoline is nearly unobtainable. Hospital patients are dying for lack of basic medical supplies. Power blackouts and water cutoffs

are endemic. As many as 4,000 businesspeople have been arrested, fined, or jailed while state-run newspapers publish lists of telephone numbers on their front pages daily, exhorting citizens to report merchants whose prices exceed the dictates."[68]

In response to the business owners' unwillingness to produce products or inability to pay workers, the Venezuelan Ministry established a transitory labor regime to restart the disastrous agricultural and food sector and get citizens much-needed food. The decree states that the government can forcibly move workers from their current jobs to work in the agricultural sector for a period of 60 days or more. Workers would be allowed to return to their original jobs upon completion of agricultural service.[69] This forced labor by the government amounts to nothing less than slavery. As noted earlier in this essay, under socialism, the government will determine which jobs serve the greater good of the collective whole.

In response to long bread lines and an apparent lack of food production, the Venezuelan government instituted a policy of fining any bakery that allows lines to stretch out their front door. In doing so, the head of Venezuela's National Superintendence for the Defense of Social and Economic Rights, William Contreras, believed the lines cause anxiety among citizens. He asserts the lines aren't an accurate indicator of a severe shortage of bread but rather a political *"strategy of generating anxiety."*[70]

All these actions ultimately lead to one of socialism's ultimate intoxications: dictatorship. The Supreme Court of

Venezuela, filled with allies of Venezuela's socialist president, dissolved the nation's elected legislature, allowing Venezuela's high court to write future laws. The court's ruling is the final step to a full-fledged dictatorship.[71]

Conclusion

"Government has three primary functions. It should provide for military defense of the nation. It should enforce contracts between individuals. It should protect citizens from crimes against themselves or their property. When government — in pursuit of good intentions- tries to rearrange the economy, legislate morality, or help special interests, the cost comes in the form of inefficiency, lack of motivation, and loss of freedom. Government should be a referee, not an active player."[72] ~ Milton Friedman

I conclude this essay with something Milton Friedman stated in an interview on the Donahue Show in 1979. He specified that the government has three primary functions. Taking nothing away from Mr. Friedman, I contend that four primary government functions exist. The government should provide for the national defense (military), roads, bridges, and transportation infrastructure, enforce contracts between individuals, and protect citizens from crimes against themselves or their property (police).[73] Unfortunately, when the government, in pursuit of good intentions or under the assertions of public safety, tries to reorganize the economy, legislate morality, or help special interests, it creates distortions on freedom, as noted earlier in this essay. As indicated by Friedman, the consequences of this flawed government's pursuit of good intentions will inevitably lead to inefficiency, a lack of motivation among citizens, and a loss of individual freedom. In other words, such attempts by the government to pursue good intentions will lead to socialism. Which, as seen in the clear example of Venezuela, is exceptionally grave. Not only for a country's economy but for individual freedom as well. It is clear from this essay that the government should be a non-biased referee, not an active player.[74]

Chapter 2

IDENTITY POLITICS FEELINGS OVER FACTS

"The problem isn't that Johnny can't read. The problem isn't even that Johnny can't think. The problem is that Johnny doesn't know what thinking is; he confuses it with feeling." ~ Thomas Sowell

JEAN-LUC, I SAT ON my patio, watching the news and contemplating the current state of race relations in America. As I sat there wondering just how we have arrived at such a flashpoint in our nation, I was inundated with images of Rachel Dolezal proclaiming her transracial status and self-identity as a black woman. Now, son, you can imagine my amazement as I watched a somewhat tanned white woman demand that I now see her as a black female. As I further listened to her ridiculous and ill-conceived justification for her living a counterfeit life as a black woman for several years and the unintended consequences of being caught, my mind went to your grandmother and aunt and how they must feel. The next thought that occurred to me was if there is so much white privilege, why would she, a white woman, pretend to be black?

Before I delve into this voluminous self-identification topic, I feel it prudent to present an analogy. Like most analogies, this analogy makes several key assumptions, yet it is nevertheless most beneficial for the topic at hand. It is late August in Texas, and you and a friend are sitting outside in the 100-degree weather. You tell your friend you are hot, which is quite evident given the 100-degree temperature and your profuse sweating. Your friend, seated by your side in a bulky overcoat and winter boots, replies that he feels cold and sees snow all around. The question now becomes: do you assume there was something mentally amiss with your friend and endeavor to seek professional medical attention for him, or would you appease his delusion of snow and cold, accept it as reality, grab your winter apparel, and join in the slow march toward dehydration and maybe death. While this analogy may seem simplistic in its construct, it is formidable in what it communicates. Just because someone feels a certain way does not make it a fact. Further, accepting those feelings as reality, even when presented with facts and evidence to the contrary, can lead to their demise and yours as well. This is the foundation from which to view this essay.

Identity Politics

There is an abundance of significant issues threatening America today, and none is more destructive to freedom than identity politics. Individual feelings and a lack of restraint are all inputs of this self-indulgent issue. As I have stated in my previous essay, *"Freedom and Democratic Socialism,"* the exercise of individual freedom without restraint is entirely problematic, and identity politics is all about one's individual freedom without such restraint, wrapped around equality.

Identity politics is enormously destructive because it is entirely artificial and built on the premise of presenting one's desires or feelings over the freedoms of others, no matter the cost. Identity politics has its roots in postmodernism. Postmodernism is a relativistic system of observation and reflection that denies absolutes and objectivity. This denial of absolutes and objectivity is replaced with one's limited subjective self-awareness and is grounded on a self-serving concept, which is filled with egalitarian undertones and seeks socialistic ends. That self-serving egalitarian motivation alone perverts the democratic process and erodes the very individual freedom the movement promises to foster.

> *"…democratic process surrounding individual, political, and economic freedoms provide socialist beliefs the precise foothold needed to continue to pursue the very reduction of those freedoms. Socialists generally exploit this democratic process, claiming to fight for more freedom or equality…."*[75] ~ *Gregory Parker.*

Identity politics flourish under the democratic process; however, at times, it undermines it.[76] Such politics foster fraud by outwardly portraying the ideas of individualism and freedom while concealing its true objective of socialism and servitude. Those pushing the activism of self-identification use emotion to create a false argument for equality while outright negating any accurate facts that do not support their narrative. Moreover, it is not at all uncommon for advocates of identity politics to literally ignore facts and basic science in their quest for equality. Such advocates proclaim the science and facts of the issue don't matter or are irrelevant.

Further, they assert the facts of the issue are racist and oppressive because those facts impede the so-called greater good of self-identification and equality. This ignoring of facts and basic science is clearly seen, as advocates believe in a genetic and biological foundation for homosexuality, while science has found no evidence for such belief. In a recent survey, as many as 70 percent of sociologists consider this unfounded acceptance plausible.[77] Likewise, in that survey, only 43 percent of those same sociologists accepted the apparent facts of biological differences between males and females. Leading one to conclude that it doesn't matter how much factual or biological evidence of differences between men and women is produced. Such disparities between the sexes will continue to be attributed to discrimination.[78]

This ignoring of absolutes, objectivity, facts, and science is also pushed by university professors, as evident by a report published in January 2016 by the University of North

Dakota's Laura Parson. Parson argues that knowledge in the science, technology, engineering, and math (STEM) fields should be seen and *"constructed by the student and dynamic, subject to change as it would in a more feminist view."*[79] Consequently, Parson does not want science to be determined and interpreted by the evidence and facts but by whatever the student wants it to mean. Parson asserts that STEM fields promote an unchanging view of knowledge, which reinforces the larger male-dominant view of knowledge because of the use of adverbs to imply certainty, such as "actually" and "in fact."[80] Although she plainly admits no overt references to gender or race in the STEM fields, Parson alleges that teaching practices and views about knowledge are inherently discriminatory to women and minorities.[81]

In another example of just how much the ignoring of absolutes, objectivity, facts, and science has taken over academia, a peer-reviewed academic journal, the Cogent Social Sciences, published a 3,000-word paper entitled *"The Conceptual Penis As A Social Construct,"* which argued that male genitals are a social construct and cause climate change.[82] The article was written by two professors seeking to prove liberal bias in academic journals. The professors cited nonexistent journals and false research and used the latest social justice jargon to create a paper with little or no substance. The professors stated that the paper *"..was rooted in moral and political biases masquerading as rigorous academic theory. Working in a biased environment, we successfully sugarcoated utter nonsense with a combination of fashionable moral sentiments and impenetrable jargon."*[83] The Cogent Social Sciences, now exposed for its liberal social justice bias and publishing a worthless paper, concluded *"The Conceptual Penis as a Social Construct' should not have been published on its merits because it was actively written to avoid having any merits whatsoever. The paper is academically worthless nonsense. The question that now needs to be answered is, How can we restore the reliability of the peer-review process?'"*[84]

University students have also learned to ignore absolutes and objective facts from these professors. Several black students from Pomona and Claremont Colleges have declared free speech and object truth to be racist. *"Historically, white supremacy has venerated the idea of objectivity and wielded a dichotomy of 'subjectivity vs. objectivity' as a means of silencing oppressed peoples. The idea that there is a single truth–' the Truth'– is a construct of the Euro-West that is deeply rooted in the Enlightenment, which was a movement that also described Black and Brown people as both subhuman and impervious to pain. This construction is a myth, and white supremacy, imperialism, colonization, capitalism, and the United States of America are all of its progeny. The idea that the truth is an entity for which we must search, in matters that endanger our abilities to exist in open spaces, is an attempt to silence oppressed peoples."*[85]

In the STEM fields, results and facts absolutely matter. One cannot envision that an engineer's designs for a new space vehicle or a high-rise building are left to their interpretations based on the engineer's political bias and feeling rather than mathematical certainties. I contend this level of advocacy for ignoring facts and science is on the order of anti-intellectualism.

> *"Intellectual honesty demands that we accept facts that we would sometimes like to wish away. Hard truths are truths nonetheless..."*[86] ~ *Jim Nelson Black.*

These anti-intellectual advocates feel they have the right to be offended by, protest against, and comment on everything that does not support their ideas by dragging down any opposing views through personal attacks and violent confrontation, not through reasonable debate. Moreover, these same anti-intellectual advocates worship entertainment over education and self-identity over self-sacrifice.[87] Bill Keller, writing in the New York Times, argues that the anti-intellectual elitism is not an elitism of wisdom, education, experience, or knowledge but an elitism of anger. Who can be the angriest advocates? This regressive elitism has formed a standing among supporters, I.E., a pecking order or competition, with the prize going to the most offended or the most absurd. Too often, it's the elite among the anti-intellectuals and the extreme culture of anti-rationalism where critical thinking is the enemy.[88] Keller also explains that the herd mentality takes over, and the anti-intellectual advocates can become an enraged lynch mob when anyone challenges one of the mob beliefs outside the mob's self-limiting set of values.

What has given rise to these anti-intellectuals and our inability to cultivate critical thinkers? A recent study by the UCLA Children's Digital Media Center has perceived a fundamental shift in the ambitions and aspirations of children. From the decade of the 90s to the new millennium, children once dreamed of becoming doctors, lawyers, or scientists, which have ranked among the top desired careers for children. These critical-thinking professionals have been replaced by a desire to simply be famous.[89] Another reason for the rise in anti-intellectualism can be found in the declining state of education in the United States. According to the Oklahoma Council of Public Affairs, 77% of public school students didn't know that George Washington was the first President and could not name Thomas Jefferson as the person responsible for the Declaration of Independence.[90] According to the 2009 National Assessment of Educational Progress, 68% of public school children in the U.S. do not read proficiently by the time they finish third grade.[91]

This sweeping shift has created a perfect space and a fertile breeding ground for recruiting those seeking to perpetuate socialism and servitude. Self-delusion and self-indulgence are replacing critical thinking. Unwitting advocates are being created based on a hollow promise that their feelings matter and that their individual desires for themselves, no matter how absurd, must be accepted by everyone, no matter the cost of truth and authenticity. These advocates believe their subjective personal versions of reality are somehow equivalent to the objective truth.

A perfect example of this absurdity can be found at the University of Michigan and its Designated Pronoun Policy. Martha Pollack, the Provost and Vice President for Academic Affairs, and E. Royster Harper, Vice President for Student Affairs, informed students in an email that students could update their pronoun preference. In protest of the new politically correct action, Grant Strobl, a junior at Michigan State, settled on the designation "His Majesty," which his fellow students and professors must now address him. If professors and staff fail to use Strobl's preferred designation, they will face disciplinary action. In another example, Multnomah County Judge Amy Holmes Hehn petitioned Patrick Abbatiello from Portland, Ore., to identify as "agender" or genderless and change his name to Patch.[92] Patrick stated, *"Even gender-neutral pronouns don't feel as if they fit me. I feel no identity or closeness with any pronouns I've come across. What describes me is my name."*[93] This anti-intellectualism and lack of critical thinking are dangerous. Gender is a stated fact, not an opinion. Therefore, someone feeling genderless does not magically change the fact that they are not that sex, and further legal documents should only report facts, not feelings.

This lack of critical thinking and clear move toward self-importance by our youth makes their advocacy myopic and remarkably singular in scope. This singular myopic advocacy, in the beginning, keeps it from clashing with other advocacy groups that seek to be the dominant angry victim. Nevertheless, the long-term struggle of these advocacy groups to be the dominant victim will create conflict and cannibalism between other groups and movements. This conflict is unmistakably evident as some feminists feel the push for transgender acceptance comes at the expense of everything the feminist crusade has fought. Actress Rose McGowan articulated her concern about transgender and former Olympic athlete Bruce Jenner, who was named Glamour Magazine's Woman of the Year, despite the well-defined fact Jenner is not a woman. *"You're a woman now? Well, fucking learn that we have had a very different experience than your life of male privilege. Being a woman comes with a lot of baggage—the weight of unequal history. You'd do well to learn it. You'd do well to wake up. Woman of the year? Not by a long fucking shot."*[94] We can see from McGowan's comments that her concern for the counterfeit social class distinction given to men who seek the pretense of being a woman, yet not having gone through the struggles of a true woman, apparently struck a chord. Feminist icon Germaine Greer stated in an interview with the BBC that trans women were not real women, *"Just because you lop off your dick and then wear a dress doesn't make you a fucking woman. I've asked my doctor to give me long ears and liver spots, and I'm going to wear a brown coat, but that won't turn me into a fucking cocker spaniel."*[95] These and other conflicts between the two advocacy groups reveal a harsh understanding of the order of victimhood in the self-identification culture. McGowan later stated that she removed the comments after facing continual accusations of transphobia. Greer faced a petition signed by thousands to stop her from delivering a lecture at Cardiff University because her views were trans-phobic.

Further fueling the constant conflict and cannibalism between these two groups is the fact that men masquerading as women feel left out of the feminist movement. A male going by the name of Jade Lejeck stated, *"I believe there's a lot of inequality that has to do with genitals — that's not something you can separate from the feminist movement. But I feel like I've tried to get involved in feminism, and there's always been a blockade there for trans women."*[96] He believes the conflict stems from the fact that feminists do not see him and others like him as true women because they have male genitals. He further stated that he did not attend the women's march for the same reasons. *"The main reason I decided not to go was because of the pussy hats, I get that they're a response to the 'grab them by the pussy' thing, but I think some people fixated on it the wrong way."*[97]

These relatively predictable circumstances and clashes are noticeably ironic, given that feminists have been pushing for the emasculation of men and boys. As evidenced by just one of many articles in the New York Times. The latest by Laurie Frankel, entitled *"From He to She in First Grade,"* Frankel waxed nostalgic about buying skirts and dresses for her son to wear to grade school.[98] Nevertheless, feminists are now angry that men are currently desiring to be considered women and achieving the emasculation they have been yearning for.

In another clash, Maya Dillard Smith, interim director of the American Civil Liberties Union (ACLU) Georgia chapter, quit after taking her elementary school-age daughters into a women's restroom, when shortly after that, three men over six feet tall with deep voices, claiming to be women entered the restroom. Smith stated, *"My children were visibly frightened, concerned about their safety, and left asking lots of questions for which I, like many parents, was ill-prepared to answer."*[99] Smith quickly faced scorn and ridicule for her concerns. A biological male who claims to be a woman named Cheryl Courtney-Evans called Dillard Smith a *"lazy"* and *"ill-educated"* woman. He further stated, *"Smith sounds like a TERF (Trans Exclusionary Radical Feminist), but maybe she's just a transphobic idiot, who was mistakenly put in a position she didn't need to fill, anymore that a homo-/trans-phobic doctor/minister needs to head up an AIDS prevention treatment organization [couldn't be trusted to do his or her best for us]. I'm glad she didn't fly under the radar as she torpedoed efforts by other ACLU members!"*[100] One has to wonder who is the absolute idiot, the man masquerading as a woman or the woman who realizes the truth. This clash also engulfed another liberal woman, Kristen Quintrall Lavin, who runs a blog called *"The Get Real Mom."* Lavin changed her views when an enormous, burly man in a Lakers Jersey entered a woman's restroom at Disneyland and began leaning against the wall. Lavin described seeing the other women and children just staring at the man, wondering what he was doing in the women's restroom, and how their collective politically correct silence, even though they knew something was wrong, caused her to tell her story. *"This notion that we're shamed into silence b/c we might offend someone has gone too far. There was a man in the bathroom. Not transgender. There was a man who felt entitled to be in the women's restroom because he knew no one would say anything.*"[101]

In yet another clash, two Canadian women were kicked out of a homeless shelter to make room for a man claiming to be a transgender woman. One of the women stated to Canada's Global News, *"I was uncomfortable with my roommate being transgender; he wants to become a woman. I mean, that is his choice, but when a man comes into a women's shelter who still has a penis and genitals, he has more rights than we do."*[102] Canada has willingly embraced the erroneous construct that biological absolutes are subordinate to gender identity relativism, so much so that the government enforces it. This enforcement has undoubtedly led to an erosion of single-sex heterosexual institutions, such as single-sex sports leagues, single-sex amenities in K-12 schools, and women's shelters, placing common sense, safety, and woman's rights in conflict with transgenderism.

Furthermore, these conflicts between identity groups also produce advocacy that delegitimizes the scope and activism of one another. The singularity of the identity groups' advocacy does not allow for a holistic visualization outside their precondition identity or ideas. For example, the delusional push to declare oneself as non-binary or gender-neutral creates a significant flaw in the very core of feminism. This glaring flaw is that one cannot have feminism or gender inequality if gender is nonexistent or fluid. A woman can simply identify as a man and lay waste to the very argument of sexism or gender pay inequality.

In addition to the conflict between identity groups, this myopic advocacy produces ridiculous and ill-conceived justifications for violent or non-violent unlawful behavior. For example, the shooting of Michael Brown, a black man, by a white cop gripped the nation. The false narrative that Michael Brown was holding his hands up in a sign of surrender before he was shot was a false flag, a lie that most blacks united behind. Even though this account was proven erroneous, it did not deter blacks from rioting after the verdict of "not guilty" was returned on behalf of the white cop.

The ridiculous and ill-conceived justification for such riots and unlawful behavior range the spectrum from "blacks just couldn't take the killing anymore," or "blacks are inherently violent, so it just happens," or "rich people are not giving them enough money, so they burn down their neighborhoods in protest." Without a doubt, the myopic advocacy of being black is the single issue that produced a ridiculous, pre-packaged, and ill-conceived justification for the violence. Moreover, those excusing the unlawful behavior of blacks clearly do not see blacks as equals. Instead, they see blacks as children unable to control their use or abuse of freedom; as I have stated before, the exercise of individual freedom without restraint is problematic at best.[103] In another example of anti-intellectuals using feeling over facts, some feel healthcare and abortion are rights covered by the Constitution even though the Constitution has no reference to either. Nevertheless, the same individuals feel no citizens should have access to or own firearms, which is clearly prominent in the Constitution as the

Second Amendment. While this latter example does not correlate with identity politics, it does, however, serve the broader point that anti-intellectual advocates' feelings over clear facts have come to infiltrate all issues in the modern era.

Further, this myopic advocacy gives rise to a cult-like mentality among its advocates. Advocates, as well as the movement, will show visible cult warning signs. According to Rick Ross, Expert Consultant and Intervention Specialist of the Cult Education Institute (CEI) and author of the book 'Cults Inside and Out,' there are ten warning signs of a potential cult and or people involved in such a group. Ross also pointed out that cultic movements or groups place considerable emphasis on feelings and emotions and that the coercive persuasion exhibited by the leaders leads to the breakdown of critical and independent thinking by its members. *"Subjectivism is sometimes linked to anti-intellectualism, putting down rational processes and devaluing knowledge and education."*[104] This sounds vastly like the myopic advocacy groups of identity politics. While I acknowledged 5 of the warning signs out of Ross's ten are seamless to my point, it is to be noted that all identity advocacy groups exhibit these warning signs over the long-term existence of the movement. It also must be understood that most cults are not based on religion; they are based on an idea and primarily focused on the financial exploitation of their members.

The first cult warning sign involves the individual's identity, and the group's identity becomes increasingly blurred; i.e., the follower's mind and group's identity become fused. This fusing can be seen with the homosexual or transgender identity movements, where it is nevertheless all the more critical being known and celebrated as a homosexual or transgender rather than for any notable accomplishments. Jeff Herbst, a former alderman, road commissioner, and mayor pro tempore, was appointed mayor of a small Texas town. All major print and television news outlets celebrated, not because of the appointment or innovative solutions Mr Herbst created to benefit the town's citizens. He was celebrated for the fact that he lived out his dilution of being a woman or transgender.[105] As is evident from not just this example but from several other examples too numerous to list in the confines of this essay, the media establishes a person is distinguished by their sexuality or gender identity, i.e., being the first gay or the first transgender, rather than the notable achievement itself.

The next cult warning sign is whenever the group is criticized or questioned; such questioning is characterized as persecution. Anyone questioning the advocacy's existence or the group's motives, even with facts or sound data, becomes an enemy and inflicts abuse on the members of the group. The group intern cries persecution through racism or some form of phobia accusation against the accuser. Whether warranted or not, these allegations are intended to make others forgo analysis or condemnation for fear of being labeled as the persecutor of those seeking equality.

The third cult warning sign is that former followers are at best-considered negative or, at worse, evil and under bad influences. Former members are not to be trusted, and personal contact by current members is to be avoided at all costs. It is noted among the transgender movement that those who 'de-transition' or decide to return to their birth gender and forgo the dilution are ostracized and outcasts as traders. The same can be said of the homosexual movement as well. A gay man was criticized for no longer engaging in the gay lifestyle. According to some gay bloggers and editors of gay publications, he was an *"Anti-gay-but-still-gay, self-hating, internalizing homophobe."*[106]

The fourth cult warning sign is a dramatic loss of spontaneity and sense of humor. Notable comedians are increasingly being attacked for jokes others claim to be offensive. There is no doubt the offbeat racial comedy of David Chappell would be enormously upsetting by today's "let no one be offended" standard. The younger generation's concerns do not amuse comedians such as Jerry Seinfeld and Monty Python member John Cleese with identity politics. Seinfeld thinks this political correctness is hurting comedy. *"They just want to use these words; that's racist. That's sexist. That's prejudice. They don't know what the f--k they're talking about."*[107] John Cleese echoed Seinfeld's statement, *"All humor is critical, If you start to say, 'We mustn't; we mustn't criticize or offend them, then humor is gone."*[108]

> *"…we demonize comedians for use of language or terminology is unspeakable. Because that's exactly what comedians should be doing: offending and upsetting people and being offensive.*

Comedy is there, like art, to make people uncomfortable, and challenge their views, and hopefully have a spirited yet civil argument. If you're a comedian whose bread and butter seems to be language, situations, and jokes that I find racist and offensive, I won't buy tickets to your show or watch you on TV. I will not support you. If people ask me what I think, I will say you suck and that I think you are racist and offensive. But I'm not going to try to put you out of work. I'm not going to start a boycott or a hashtag, looking to get you driven out of the business."[109]

The fifth cult warning sign involves the group having no tolerance for questions or critical inquiry, i.e., no tolerance for critical thinking within the group. The movement or group and its leaders have a vested interest in keeping its members devoid of facts or critical thought. The more anti-intellectual the members, the easier they are to control. This lack of critical thinking is most evident in the transgender and black lives matter movements, where basic facts and critical thinking would undoubtedly confirm the groups to be delusional and pointless.

With all that said, we will now explore a few of the issues of identity politics within the scope of this essay. It is to note that I by no means claim to have all the answers, nor do I possess the remedy for stopping the cancer that is identity politics. To follow is my humble understanding of the issue and a brief examination of what I believe to be the major fraudulent issues within identity politics facing the modern age.

Transgender Politics

The anti-intellectual, self-absorbed thought that one's gender is fluid and open to choice has saturated our society in recent years. Son, this 'transgender' movement is a clear illustration of anti-intellectual advocacy and the outright antithetical position to any facts and basic science. All in an effort to give societal acceptance to a mental disorder enveloped in a socialist theory.

> *"The Democrat Party declares that a man exercises total agency over his own biology and that citizens should be forced by law to recognize and affirm his self-centered delusions."*[110] ~ *Matt Walsh*

Transgender is socially defined as a person whose gender identity does not correspond to that person's biological sex assigned at birth. Transgenderism is a mental disorder for which the official psychological term is Gender dysphoria, a condition of feeling one's emotional and psychological identity to be opposite to one's biological sex --- conflict between a person's physical or assigned gender and the gender with which they identified.[111] It is somewhat noteworthy that the literal psychological definition of gender dysphoria states that one's 'feelings' are in conflict with facts. This mental disorder is not unlike bipolar, depression, or schizophrenia and often makes one feel something that isn't true, even if the person affected cannot determine the distinction. Given that gender fluidity is scientifically impossible, transgenderism is a self-deception and is based on a single flawed assumption that one's sexual nature (feelings) is misaligned with one's biological sex (fact). This single faulty assumption, combined with the political freedom to push for equality for those with perplexed feelings about their gender, has led to a socialist movement around this lie.

Political leaders have not missed this blatant disregard for facts by the transgender movement. Supporters such as former President Obama, believing transgenderism is a civil rights issue, used an executive order to direct US public schools, through the U.S. Justice and Education Departments, to let transgender students use the bathrooms and locker rooms that match their gender identity or the gender they feel at that moment.[112] This push has given anti-intellectuals within the transgender movement more credence to ignore the basic scientific fact that human bodies are either male or female and that males are physically different than females. This is evident as a school in Alaska allowed a male athlete to compete with females in the state track and field championships. The mother of one of the girls who lost to the transgender runner stated, *"We had no idea she was running against a male until after the race was over. How do you explain to her that not only does she need to train to beat her fellow female athletes now she should also train to beat the males?"*[113] Additionally, the Northern New Jersey Council of the Boy Scouts of America allowed a nine-year-old girl whose parents were masquerading her around as a boy into a New Jersey

Cub Scout pack. According to administrative court documents, the Northern New Jersey Council agreed to pay $18,000 to the girl's parents and issue an apology for previously excluding her from the cub pack.[114]

The blatant disregard for biological facts doesn't go without praise from sports networks. Chris Mosier, a New York-based woman, claiming to be a male athlete, who became the first transgender person to pose for ESPN's Body issue, pronounced that *"Trans inclusion is the next frontier in athletic equality."*[115] Further evidence that such advocates proclaim the science and facts of the issue are oppressive because those facts impede the so-called greater good of self and equality.

Proponents also believe that altering their bodies to match their current feelings might be the answer. This altering does more damage than good. According to a study conducted out of Sweden, a culture strongly supportive of the transgender movement, those having gender reassignment surgery, over time, continue to have lifelong mental unrest. Ten to fifteen years after gender reassignment surgery, suicide rates rose to twenty times that of comparable peers.[116] Dr. Paul R. McHugh, the Distinguished Service Professor of Psychiatry at Johns Hopkins University and former psychiatrist-in-chief at Johns Hopkins Hospital, who has studied transgenderism and sex-reassignment surgery for 40 years, stated that the better course of treatment should be aimed at the psychological rather than the surgical.

Moreover, Dr. Joseph Berger, a prominent Canadian psychiatrist, echoed Dr. Paul R. McHugh in his comments to the Canadian House of Commons Standing Committee on Justice and Human Rights, "*Scientifically, there is no such a thing [as transgendered]. Therefore, anyone who actually truly believes that notion is, by definition, deluded psychotic. The medical treatment of delusions or psychosis is not by surgery.*"[117]

Furthermore, with as many as 98% of gender-confused boys and 88% of gender-confused girls eventually accepting their biological sex after naturally passing through puberty, the American College of Pediatricians issued a statement condemning gender reclassification in children stating that transgenderism in children amounts to child abuse.[118] "*The American College of Pediatricians urges educators and legislators to reject all policies that condition children to accept as normal a life of chemical and surgical impersonation of the opposite sex. Facts – not ideology – determine reality.*"

Dr. Stephen Stathis, one of Australia's top Psychiatrists on gender, stated in an article for the Courier Mail that adolescents are trying out being transgender to stand out or gain attention from their peers. Dr. Stathis quoted one patient as saying, "*Dr. Steve ... I want to be transgender, it's the new black*',"[119] Even the self-described liberal group Youth Trans Critical Professionals expressed concern about the trendiness of today's youth being transgender. The group believes the current trend to quickly diagnose and affirm young people as transgender is problematic and often sets young people down a path toward medical transition.[120]

"Our concern is with medical transition for children and youth. We feel that unnecessary surgeries and/or hormonal treatments which have not been proven safe in the long term represent significant risks for young people. Policies that encourage — either directly or indirectly — such medical treatment for young people who may not be able to evaluate the risks and benefits are highly suspect, in our opinion."[121]

"People who encourage very young kids to act out, switch genders, and live a life of pretend need to understand...[the child]..could be suffering from a dissociative disorder, just as happened with me. My feelings of not wanting to be a boy started in early childhood as a result of cross-dressing at the hands of my grandma,"[122] were the comments made by Walt Heyer, an author and public speaker, who himself impersonated a female for eight years until he completed university studies in the field of psychology. Upon reflection of his years of masquerading, he stated, "I had discovered the madness of the transgender life. It is a fabrication born of mental disorders."[123]

So opponents of the transgender movement in Texas, Arkansas, and elsewhere vowed defiance and subsequently proposed 'bathroom' bills to restrict transgender people from using bathrooms and locker rooms of their birth gender. US Congressman Louie Gohmert (R-TX) echoed something I have said many times, "I have come to find out there is one science that supports the transgender agenda, political science."[124] Society at large should not accommodate this delusion of

transgenderism by pretending to accept it as reality.
A deluded person is not treated by requiring everyone who
encounters them to accept the validity of their delusion,
contrary to all reality.[125]

Society at large does not accept the accurate idea of
changing one's gender. According to a survey conducted by
Ipsos for the Williams Institute, a pro-transgender advocacy
group at the University of California at Los Angeles, 77.3
percent of people surveyed believe people should not be
allowed to change their biological sex on government
documents, especially given that only an estimated 0.04
percent of the population identifies as transgender.[126] As Dr.
Paul R. McHugh stated in an article he wrote for Public
Discourse, transgendered men do not become women, nor do
transgendered women become men. All become counterfeits
or impersonators of the sex with which they identify.[127] Dr.
Joseph Berger stated in his comments to the Canadian House
of Commons Standing Committee on Justice and Human
Rights that cosmetic surgery will not change the
chromosomes of a human being in so much that it will not
make a man become a woman, capable of menstruating, nor
will it make a woman into a man, capable of generating
sperm.[128]

The media and transgender advocacy groups are
demanding to elevate the false narrative of transgenderism.
However, I see a critical juncture for society. History is
cyclical, and a clear pattern exists in all ancient cultures. As
society begins to decline, the rise of the transgender

movement becomes more prominent.[129] In other words, the rise of the transgender movement is a symptom or precursor to the cultural collapse of all ancient civilizations.

Further, British scholar C.E.M. Joad found in his study entitled 'Decadence' that a society's preoccupation with self and self-identity is a sign of the decline of a civilization.[130] As we can see from the wanton embrace of cultural Marxism or what is commonly known as political correctness, we are in the midst of a downward cultural collapse. To see just how convoluted and ridiculous this gender-fluid delusion has become, we will review a few examples of this cult-like identity movement.

A woman pretending to be a man transitioned in her early 20s by taking testosterone, changing her legal name, and having chest surgery to remove her breasts. Given that she identifies as a man, her husband, a biological man, is considered to be her gay partner. The two wanted to have and "chest-feed" a child. Of her situation, she stated, *"I was worried that breastfeeding might feel gendered to me – I thought, am I going to be able to do that, or am I going to experience a lot of gender dysphoria?"*[131] Given the anti-intellectual nature of this situation, I can only assume she does not realize she has been experiencing gender dysphoria the entire time. Further, it appears from her statement that she was concerned about feeling normal. Moreover, while fighting the feeling of biological normalcy, she found an incredibly convoluted way to arrive at the exact normal relationship between a man and a woman she was trying to avoid.

I have always felt *"little," which* is the explanation a 21-year-old woman gives for identifying and living like a baby. She engages in regressive activities, like wearing diapers and baby clothing, because it feels comforting. She says that she was abused as a two-year-old, and this is a way to help cope with the trauma.[132] Moreover, a Canadian man, married with seven kids, left his family in order to fulfill what he asserts was his true identity and now lives as a 6-year-old girl. He claims he realized he was transgender, rather than simply cross-dressing and split from his wife after she told him to discontinue the delusion or leave.

Further, Rodney James Quine, a 57-year-old convicted killer serving a life sentence in a California male prison, became the first U.S. inmate to receive state-funded sex reassignment surgery. Kris Hayashi, executive director of the Transgender Law Center, which represents transgender inmates, stated, *"For too long, institutions have ignored doctors and casually dismissed medically necessary and life-saving care for transgender people just because of who we are."*[133] State officials have now received 64 inmate requests for sex-reassignment surgeries, with four having now been approved.[134] Since the sex-reassignment surgery, Quine has been moved to a female prison unit, where he now describes his current placement as being "torture," pointing to the fact that he is isolated from other offenders and has no access to a razor. Further, Quine also has a history of suicide attempts.[135]

A female enrolled at Wellesley College, an all-female college, decided to masquerade as a white male named

Timothy. She pressed the administration and other students to use male pronouns and see her as a man. This attempt to force the transgender delusion onto others was so successful that when she decided to run for Diversity Officer of the college, the student body rallied against her. One student summed up the student body's feelings with this statement: *"It's not just about that position... having men in elected leadership positions undermines the idea of this being a place where women are the leaders."*[136] The student body's feelings are interesting given that 'Timothy' is neither a male nor white.

Self-indulgence and enabling are clear byproducts of political correctness on steroids. Jean-Luc, one may believe that the examples above are improbable, yet they are entirely possible, and I believe a compliant media corrupted by a socialist agenda fuels such delusional behavior. A former Olympian, hero, and role model to a generation of boys and young men is now an icon of the transgender delusion. Fast forward to the young men of today and the role models they see. There is a 17-year-old boy who has just been named CoverGirl's new CoverBoy, which was once limited to celebrity women of beauty. Enabling self-indulgent delusional behavior while demonizing rational reasoning is now pervasive in our modern era, and it is a manipulative tool that leads to socialism and servitude.

Gregory E. Parker

Transracial Politics: The New Blackface

America is quite familiar with the complex racial and
ethnic makeup of cities and families from before slavery
through this modern age. Nevertheless, a new, for lack of a
better word, phenomenon called "Transracial" has reached
into the modern consciousness. I am hesitant to say new, but
to this millennial generation, this word will suffice, given the
unfamiliarity with previous concepts.

Transracial is when a person, born of one race, makes the
decision to change their outward appearance, using tanning
or makeup, and represent him or herself as another race. This
essay will suggest this modern definition is nothing more
than an innovative package for the old narrative of blackface.
Now, before I start, it is imperative that I explain the term
blackface and its origin for those unfamiliar with the concept.

Blackface, as defined by Merriam-Webster dictionary, is
makeup applied to a performer playing a black person,
especially in a minstrel show. It originated in the 1820s when
white men, during minstrel shows, would portray plantation-
enslaved people and free blacks. The minstrel shows,
associated with blackface, were very popular from the 1820s
to the 1890s. The performers used caricatures to mock blacks,
which eventually became ingrained ugly stereotypes of blacks
in the US. Jim Crow and Zip Coon became two of the most
famous examples of blackface. Other popular characters in
minstrel shows include the mammy, a heavyset black woman
faithful to her master, and the Buck, an intimidating black

man who adored white women. The pickaninny, black children with unkempt hair. Uncle Tom is a black man devoted to white ideals, and the wench is a black temptress.[137]

From the 1880s to the early 1930s, Vaudeville was a genre of theater for blackface. This method of show had become so ingrained with white audiences that most declined to accept black performers unless they performed in blackface. Black performer William Henry Lane, a tap dancer, performed in blackface until he became so well-known that he was granted permission to perform as a black man without black makeup.[138] In 1938 two years before she became synonymous with The Wizard Of Oz, Judy Garland performed in blackface as a pickaninny in the movie Everybody Sing.[139] As recently as 1986, the movie *"Soul Man"* was about a privileged white college student masquerading as a black man to win a Harvard Law School scholarship. This portrayal appears to be the unfortunate reality as of late. *"Tropic Thunder"* (2008) is a movie where Robert Downey Jr. plays a white method actor who undergoes pigmentation alteration surgery in order to appear black to play a black army sergeant. Country star Jason Aldean dressed as rapper Lil Wayne in a Halloween costume. His representative confirmed the outfit after a photo surfaced of Aldean wearing blackface makeup and a wig with dreadlocks.[140]

In the modern era, blackface has not faded. It has morphed into the transracial issue. If we overlay the two definitions, we can see the striking similarities. When a person, born of one race (white man or woman), decides to change their outward appearance, using tanning or makeup (blackface performers used makeup), and represent him or herself as another race (play a black person), especially in a minstrel show.

Since I contend transracial is the new blackface, let's look at a few examples. Shaun King and Rachel Dolezal were leaders of the groups BLM & NAACP, respectively. It is evident the pair put on blackface every day and perform modern-day minstrel shows, dancing and singing the tune of victimization to keep blacks on the plantation of mediocrity and ignorance.

In 2015, Rachel Dolezal, at the time the head of the NAACP's Spokane, Washington chapter, was exposed as a white woman who donned a tan (blackface) and frizzy hairpieces to falsely represent herself as a black woman. Overnight, a blizzard of media coverage and interviews forced America to deal with Dolezal's narcissistic charade. Dolezal's response to the media firestorm came in an interview on the talk show *"The Real,"* where she stated her feelings over facts: *"I was biologically born white, but I identify as black."*[141] This is ironic given the fact that in 2002, Dolezal sued the historically black university of which she was a student for discrimination. Dolezal, then known as Rachel Moore, claimed the university discriminated based on race and gender by removing some of her artworks from a student exhibition in favor of a black student's artwork.[142] Sincere Kirabo, writing for the Humanist news magazine, stated: *"Dolezal is a living embodiment of all the conceit, self-indulgence, insensibility, and intellectual malpractice..."*[143]

In 2015, Shaun King, a prominent activist for the Black Lives Matter and the Justice Together movements was discovered to be white as well. King's answer after the discovery was, *"I am biracial."*[144] He has continually maintained that response even after a media blitz proving otherwise. King was scrutinized by 30 of his Justice Together state directors for questionable dealings with Justice Together finances. The 30 published an open letter pointing out discrepancies between King's public persona and the man behind the computer screen.[145] The group noted, *"He silenced dissent without productive discussion, he removed volunteers for speaking up due to his self-proclaimed paranoia, he repeatedly failed to meet his own timelines for his participation in the work, and he failed to delegate or discuss internally anything of consequence within the organization."*[146] King later dissolved the organization but is still active within the movement. It appears BLM refuses to speak about the issue. *"Many of us chose not to speak publicly about our disappointment with JTA's dissolution and King's mishandling of the organization because we know the forces of white supremacy will attempt to exploit such disagreements to delegitimize the movement for black lives."*[147]

Joshua Marcus, a Joburg-based freelance writer and copywriter for the Huffington Post, claims he no longer identifies as white because his male partner is not white. He stated in his article that he is white and very Jewish, but *"he can't help but feel that his racial and cultural identity has changed because his boyfriend is mixed race."*[148] Joshua Marcus also

69

describes himself as a confused liberal and lover of life. I would say confused is indeed suitable.

With these modern-era examples of blackface, there are still those that excuse their behavior by claiming racism doesn't exist but that race itself is only a social construct created by slavery. Writer Steven Thrasher noted in his article in the Guardian News that *"Race is a fiction—which has only existed as we presently conceive it over the past few hundred years since European colonialism and American chattel slavery began peddling its mythology. But despite being a fiction, its effects are so real in our lives that it can be difficult to imagine ourselves outside our present hell.*[149] The ridiculousness of this statement cannot be analyzed within the confines of this essay, but with such an ill-conceived rationale, blacks could simply renounce their blackness, self-identify as white, and put an end to racial profiling or driving while black issues.[150]

Of course, given the blatant disregard for the facts and science and the myopic nature of this transracial movement, it has created conflict with other racial identity movements. The question of racial identity has triggered liberals to decry transracialism as cultural appropriation, I.E., those claiming the victim mantle of transracial are merely stealing the culture of which they claim to identify with and or are impostors of said culture. I find this genuinely ironic, given Dr. Paul R. McHugh stated in an article he wrote for Public Discourse transgendered men do not become women, nor do transgender women become men. All become counterfeits or impersonators of the sex with which they identify. Therefore, liberals are using science and logic to counter identity politics that are lower on the victim hierarchy, yet forgoing that same science and logic for others.

Questions About Black Lives Matter

On to the current phenomenon known as the Black Lives Matter movement. Although 65% of blacks support Black Lives Matter or BLM, it unmistakably fits into the realm of destructive identity politics and perpetual hypocrisy.[151] Democratic candidates for office did not miss black support points in the 2016 election cycle. Federal candidates continued to submit to BLM and its demands, even given its destructive nature. One reason for this is because the national Democrat Party warned, in a 2015 confidential memo to its federal candidates, not to use the words "all lives matter" or speak about black-on-black crime under any circumstances, given such a response may garner additional media scrutiny and only anger BLM activists. The document, intended to advise on how to deal with the Black Lives Matter movement, described BLM as a "radical movement" seeking to be part of the conversation.[152] It appears the National Democrat Party's solution when dealing with the advocacy group is clearly pacification and appeasement by ignoring obvious facts. It is worth noting that while exploring the BLM movement, their guiding principles, and political demands, I found numerous contradictions and hypocrisies within these documents.

Therefore, I was forced to narrow the scope of my reflection to keep this review within the confines of this essay.

Created in 2012, BLM proclaims it was launched in response to the death of Trayvon Martin and other black males killed. Absent from the group's guiding principles is anything remotely related to the plight of black men. Given the three female founders of BLM are community organizers and feminists, I would gather to guess they have no actual use for black men. The trio is so feminist they have even gone so far as to change the group "history" to "herstory." Black men are an inconvenient means to a socialist end. Roland C. Warren noted in his op-ed in the Washington Times, *"If you objectively read the Black Lives Matter movement principles, you will quickly notice that most of them have nothing to do with the issues facing the black community and, certainly, not the black men and boys that the group has used as 'martyrs' to gain a national voice. Moreover, as you read the principles, you will not find a single reference to black men and boys, except for trans men, which are men who want to be considered women."*[153] This was quite telling, given the socialist construct of equality for blacks, black males in particular, is the constant narrative the group feeds the national media.

BLM's advocacy is very narrow-minded and remarkably singular in its scope. Such bigotry can be plainly seen in a quick review of the group's guiding principles. One of the group's principles declares they strive to be unapologetically black, and they need not say why; *"We are unapologetically Black in our positioning. In affirming that Black Lives Matter, we need not qualify our position...*" yet in a similar fashion, they also assert to strive for diversity; "*We are committed to acknowledging, respecting and celebrating difference(s) and commonalities.*"[154] With the definition of diversity literally having many different forms, types, ideas, races, and or cultures in a group or organization, how then would it be possible for BLM to be unapologetically black yet desire diversity? The answer lies in the largely socialist underpinning of the organization.[155] I argue that being black to BLM is a fluid construct built on feeling and not facts. Moreover, whites, such as Shaun King and others, can belong and are clearly welcome as long as they are in 'blackface' and perform the minstrel songs of socialism and servitude.[156]

Moreover, if BLM is so unapologetically black, why would they not want to protect all black lives? It appears black-on-black crime and black abortions go virtually unnoticed by the group. According to FBI statistics for 2012, there were 2,648 black homicides; of those black deaths, a black person accounted for 2,412 of them.[157] Since 1973, a total of more than 13 million black babies have been aborted. On average, that is 1,876 black babies are aborted every day in America. Further, black women are five times more likely to have an abortion than white women.[158]

Some offer ridiculous and ill-conceived justifications for why BLM does not address these black lives. Segregating 'black on black' crime into its own category is another form of racism. This clearly overlooks the fact that BLM is inviting the very segregation it does not want. In addition, the BLM group believes law enforcement officers are racist and are the reincarnation of slave catchers.[159] According to a Black Lives Matter organizer, Melina Abdullah, who spoke at California State University, *"Police that we now have were the slave catchers. So that is where it comes from. You literally have a target on your back. That is what policing was founded on, and that is what it evolved out of. So the former slave catchers or paddy rollers, they were called slave patrols."*[160]

However, it is worth noting the absolute racial aspect of abortion and the history of the founder of Planned Parenthood. Margret Sanger is the "Mother" of the abortion movement. Her roots in this movement were fed by her belief in culling out the unfit and feeble with a conviction in forced sterilization. The plight of black women was described in a 1973 exposé in Essence magazine that highlighted the forced sterilization of rural black women. These sterilizations went largely unnoticed by the women until they decided to begin having children.[161] Many facts surrounding Margret Sanger and her attitudes towards eugenics are well documented yet continue to be refuted by revisionist historians. I believe that BLM does not focus on black-on-black crime or black abortions because the group would cease to be myopic or singular in its advocacy and scope. This would put BLM in conflict with the socialist principles it holds at its core.

The group's guiding principle concerning the black family is more of a rallying cry to continue its destruction. *"We are committed to disrupting the Western-prescribed nuclear family structure requirement by supporting each other as extended families and 'villages' that collectively care for one another, and especially 'our' children to the degree that mothers, parents, and children are comfortable.*"[162] Common knowledge defines a 'Western-prescribed nuclear family structure' as a married father and mother with children. With that said, instilling discipline in the children within the family has traditionally been the role of the father. However, the father is notably absent from the black family. Black children stand in distinction from any other racial group, with an astonishing 64% of black children growing up with only their mother as of 2014.

In contrast, in 1865 or prior, when black marriages were in some cases illegal, 63.5% of black children grew up with both parents in the home.[163] There are consequences to the marginalization of the father in the black family. Creating foot soldier advocates who will mindlessly follow their master and perpetuating the servant class requires creating an imbalance in the nuclear family. Father absence is linked to low academic performance, behavior problems, and risks for incarceration. The 2013 FBI Uniform Crime Report shows that black offenders killed 90 percent of black victims. The vast majority of victims and perpetrators are black men.[164]

Speaking of black fathers, while the words mother and children were used in BLM's family guiding principle, remarkably absent was the word father. So why doesn't BLM want to restore the black father to the family, reducing poverty, low scholastic performance, behavior problems, risks for incarceration, and by extension, crime? BLM is not committed to bringing black fathers back to the family unit because BLM would instead "transform" black women into men as their solution -- BLM transgender principal: *"We are committed to embracing and making space for trans brothers and sisters to participate and lead. We are committed to being self-reflexive and doing the work required to dismantle cis-gender privilege and uplift Black trans folk, especially Black trans women who continue to be disproportionately impacted by trans-antagonistic violence"*[165], or BLM's queer affirming principal *"We are committed to fostering a queer-affirming network. When we gather, we do so with the intention of freeing ourselves from the tight grip of hetero-normative thinking or, rather, the belief that all in the world are heterosexual unless s/he or they disclose otherwise."*[166]

The fraudulent movement of BLM has crossed over into England with preposterous beginnings. The Black Lives Matter UK chapter claimed responsibility for a September 6, 2016 demonstration by nine protesters. The nine white protesters shut down a London City Airport's runway. In a statement, BLM USA stated, *"We send you solidarity, as we see Mzee Mohammed. We see Sarah Reed. We see Jermaine Baker, the 1558 people killed by police in the UK, and your long struggle to gain justice for them. When you lose your family, know that we see that loss, and we feel it, too. We are ALL family."*[167] This is quite ironic given all nine of the protesters involved were from privileged backgrounds and claimed to have targeted the airport, not because of deaths related to police violence but because planes contribute to climate change, which the group claimed has a disproportionate effect on ethnic minorities.[168]

BLM's movement is undoubtedly based on the "Critical Race Theory." Critical Race Theory is a legal theory that challenges the validity of concepts such as objective truth and judicial neutrality in the context of race. This theory derives its philosophical framework from within Marxist thought or socialism. Advocates of such critical race theory argue that racism is not a matter of an individual choice, i.e., an individual cannot choose to be racist, but rather, it is embedded in American attitudes, institutions, and within white people's DNA. Consequently, you can now understand BLM's push for equality, regardless of the facts. The irony of this movement is that the Marxist theory from which it is derived is taken from Karl Marx, who himself was a racist and held a very low opinion of blacks. Marx, in correspondence to his friend Engels about his socialist political competitor Ferdinand Lassalle, Marx wrote:

> *"It is now completely clear to me that he, as is proved by his cranial formation and his hair, descends from the Negroes who had joined Moses' exodus from Egypt, assuming that his mother or grandmother on the paternal side had not interbred with a nigger. Now this union of Judaism and Germanism with a basic Negro substance must produce a peculiar product."*[169]

Separate But Equal

Dr. Martin Luther King Jr. stated in a 1964 televised speech, *"We must learn to live together as brothers, or we will all perish together as fools."* These words are very powerful and, I might add, prophetic statements against segregation. Segregation, or separate but equal, the practice or policy of keeping people of different races and religions separated from each other, is alive and well in the modern era. The doctrine of separate but equal was confirmed in the Plessy v. Ferguson Supreme Court decision of 1896 and subsequently overturned in 1954 with the Brown v. Board of Education case. However, BLM, black student unions, and black college students from across the country are now demanding that they become segregated from their white peers into "safe spaces" on campuses. Perhaps ignorance of the 1960s, where "colored only" signs proliferated the American landscape, is the reason to call for a return to segregation.

California State University Los Angeles (CSULA) joins the University of Connecticut, the University of Michigan, and other universities in offering segregated housing dedicated to black students, a move intended to protect them from "microaggressions" and provide a cheaper alternative housing solution.[170] Although the University of Connecticut has stated that it intends to improve the low 55 percent graduation rate among black men compared to the 83 percent graduation rate for all other students. Conversely, many students believe these changes the University of California has instituted are not conducive to a more inclusive campus climate. A survey conducted by undergraduate students at CSULA found that 86.67% believed CSULA's actions were not helping to raise levels of interracial tolerance on campus.[171] Most find it difficult to understand how one betters themselves through isolation.

Further, as noted in my previous essay, *"Freedom and Democratic Socialism,"* CSULA's efforts clearly distort freedom by supplementation. CSULA seeks to give equality to one group by further eroding the freedom and equality of others, which creates more inequality. Conversely, now that blacks have CSULA-sponsored affordable housing and scholarships, why shouldn't Asians, Latinos, and whites, who are now unequal, demand equivalents?

This modern era return to segregation is also evident in many on-campus events. Not surprisingly, these events are to protect students from racism yet divide the very protesters by race. At Claremont College, a speaker was shut down by an anti-racist protester. Organizers of the protest that turned violent segregated themselves by race (whites in the front and blacks in the back). The organizers stated, *"For white accomplices: Please keep in mind that your role at this protest, aside from acting in solidarity with POC students at the 5Cs, particularly Black students, is to serve as a buffer between students of color and the police. That means, if the police come, it is imperative that you stay at the protest with fellow accomplices and engage with cops should it come to that."*[172]

Black graduate students from Harvard University hosted a black-only graduation ceremony. Michael Huggins, a Harvard's Kennedy School graduate student who assisted in the ceremony, stated, "This is an opportunity to celebrate Harvard's Black excellence and *brilliance. It's an event where we can see each other, and our parents and family can see us as a collective, whole group. A community. This is not about segregation. It's about fellowship and building a community. This is a chance to reaffirm for each other that we enter the work world with a network of supporters standing with us. We are all partners.* "[173]

This effort to use self-segregation is not only seen in colleges but also in K-12 public schools as well. In Tuscaloosa, Alabama, where the city's black liberal elite facilitated, to some extent, self-segregation or resegregation among blacks, nearly one in three black students attends a school that looks as if Brown v. Board of Education never happened.[174] This self-segregation, under the fallacy and false narrative of "protecting minorities from whites," has apparently not worked regarding achieving academic excellence. Central High School was a renowned local high school in Tuscaloosa and one of the South's signature integration success stories. A few years after a federal judge ordered the merger of the city's two largely segregated high schools, Central obtained National Merit Scholarships and numerous math competition victories.

After integration, it had become, by all accounts, a powerhouse among K-12 public schools in the nation. Currently, Central High has a student body consisting of 99% black and little, if any, national awards and recognitions. Rucker Johnson, a public policy professor at the University of California at Berkeley, found in his 2014 study that black Americans who attended integrated schools were more likely to graduate, go on to college, and earn a degree than black

Americans who attended segregated schools.[175] Integrated schooling increased the earnings of black adults by 15 percent, and black adults were significantly less likely to spend time in jail.[176] In another example, the Black Lives Matter Philadelphia chapter banned white people from future meetings and official memberships in the organization. The group desires to create what can only be considered 'blacks only' space, and in their social media post, declared that if you do not identify as black, you cannot *"attend our meetings and become a member."*[177]

This effort to use self-segregation to create separate but equal accommodations is precisely what Martin Luther King and other civil rights activists fought to stop. Moreover, this movement is clearly anti-intellectual societal regression masquerading as social justice, which only serves to create envy and further racial division. It will undoubtedly hamper the very individuals the movement claims to want to assist.

Aeman Ansari noted in an article in the Huffington Post the ill-conceived justification for these so-called safe spaces. *"Segregation was imposed on people of color by people of privilege, not the other way around. The very fact that individuals organizing to help each other get through social barriers and injustices are being attacked and questioned for their peaceful assembly is proof that they were right to exclude those students. Radicalized people experience systemic discrimination on a daily basis, on many levels, and in ways that white people may never encounter. The whole point of these safe spaces is to remove that power dynamic. That's partly what makes them spaces for healing."*[178] According to Aeman

Ansari, the reason for the segregated spaces or 'blacks only' areas is because white people forced segregation on blacks in the past, so that makes it fundamentally correct for blacks to segregate themselves now voluntarily. Under this perverse rationale, it is offensive for a white person, or any person other than black, to place a 'blacks or colored only' sign up or to call for segregated spaces as it is deemed racist. However, blacks can call for segregation and place the shingle of "blacks only, " and all must comply.

The fallacy is to believe self-imposed separate by equal segregation is a new idea as of late. In fact, all races have been practicing self-segregation since before segregation was therefore outlawed. Blacks being the most notable with the National Association for the Advancement of Colored People (NAACP) created in 1909 by an interracial group consisting of W.E.B. Du Bois, Ida Bell Wells-Barnett, Mary White Ovington, in the wake of the 1908 Springfield (Illinois) Race Riot. The Japanese American Citizens League (JACL) was formed in 1930 under the banner of a civic organization dedicated to gaining acceptance for its people. Additionally, the League of United Latin American Citizens (LULAC), founded in 1929, was created to empower and develop opportunities for Latin American citizens.

Conclusion

In conclusion, whether it is BLM or any number of other identity causes, they are all built on the foundation of socialism and subjective reality, and all lead down the road to servitude. If you take anything from this essay, Jean-Luc takes away these points. 1) one's subjective version of reality is not equivalent to objective truth, 2) that all lives matter, but they must matter to all first, 3) the flawed construct of equal outcome for all can and will not be achieved, nor will it ever be won; given that everyone is different and unequal. To consider otherwise elevates feelings, discounts facts, and is a meaningless struggle of which there is no happy or equal conclusion.

Chapter 3

CAPITALISM AND MORALITY

"Socialism is a philosophy of failure, the creed of ignorance, and the gospel of envy, its inherent virtue is the equal sharing of misery" ~ Winston Churchill.

ON A WARM FALL day at a local university, I observed several students dressed in high-end summer apparel, gripping their iPhones and listening to rap music on their "Beats by Dre" headphones that dangled from their necks. They began shouting, *"Capitalism is immoral"* at the top of their lungs. With a grin and a chuckle, I began pondering the overwhelming irony and ignorance that had befallen these clearly misinformed and misguided college students.

Jean-Luc, this incident sparked a question in my mind: is capitalism immoral? While simplistic in its verbal construct, this question is yet very sophisticated in its analysis. Therefore, I felt it prudent to examine the subject of capitalism and its moral foundation. However, it is crucial to define the term morality initially. This definition will help achieve a shared understanding and a basic framework by which to evaluate the aforementioned question and the depth of this essay.

> *"All those rejecting capitalism on moral grounds as an unfair system are deluded by their failure to comprehend what capital is, how it comes into existence and how it is maintained, and what the benefits are which are derived from its employment in production processes."*[179] ~ *Ludwig von Mises.*

Morality

> *"The moral justification of capitalism lies in the fact that it is the only system consonant with man's rational nature, that it protects man's survival..."*[180] ~*Ayn Rand.*

Many in this modern era believe that capitalism is an archaic economic system built on selfishness and immorality. This question of morality can be very convoluted and never-ending. One could analyze the writings of Socrates, Aristotle, and other prominent philosophers to arrive at a very profound conclusion. However, I have elected to take a less complicated assessment of the term. Webster's Dictionary defines immoral as not good or not right, conflicting with generally or traditionally held moral principles. David Kendall stated in his book, *"Morality and Capitalism,"* that moral behavior is the proper conduct for humans when interacting with other humans. Moreover, morality is a prescriptive code that all rational people agree governs the conduct of all other reasonable people.

An example would be an investment banker who knows that taking millions of dollars from his customers is wrong, thereby destroying their savings, but does it anyway. All clearly recognize stealing is wrong and will demand actions be taken. Therefore, I assert that being immoral is having no morality or good and that one knows what society considers right and wrong, yet one does wrong despite that knowledge.

It should also be noted that this morality cannot be coerced. If morality is forced rather than voluntary, morality is therefore lacking. For example, if an investor donates money to feed people experiencing poverty, one would claim that action is moral; however, if the investment banker steals money from the investor, then donates it to people experiencing poverty on the investor's behalf. Subsequently, morality is, therefore, absent and is not considered moral and virtuous, given the actions are coercive. Coercing individuals to purchase or sell a product negates morality and the capitalistic intent. This false virtuosity or economics by coercion has clear and overwhelming evidence against its use, yet there are a number of economists who subscribe to the theory of nationalization of industry, wage and price controls, confiscatory taxation, and even outright abolition of private property as a good thing.[181] Additionally, to steal, limit, or tax one individual under the assertion of the public or moral good in an effort to assist one single individual or a select group is not moral or virtuous; it is theft.

With that said, we can undoubtedly reason the layer of individualism within this morality definition, i.e., the individual's freedom to choose to be moral or good. The individual investment banker has to decide to act immorally and has the freedom to make that choice. Further, given that capitalism is an economic system built on individual freedom to choose, it gives one a clear understanding that the individual is immoral, not the entire system. However, opponents of capitalism in this modern era will, incorrectly, of course, look at the system collectively when making a judgment as to whether capitalism is immoral. As noted above, the example of the investment banker, opponents of capitalism who see a flawed system, not a flawed individual, would spark a rallying cry for lawmakers to create more regulation on all within the economic system rather than simply punishing the immoral individual. Thereby, they mistakenly pursue distortions on freedom through reduction.[182] Therefore, for the purpose of this essay, it is necessary for me to fashion some level of collective standard moral criteria by which to judge capitalism. Conversely, I will use poverty, greed, and envy, i.e., does capitalism increase poverty and foster greed and envy? These and other fallacies will be examined later in this essay.

It should also be noted that this essay is not an exhaustive look at this subject, nor should it be viewed as such. What follows are my humble opinions on the topic of capitalism, given my research.

What is Capitalism

In the mixed economy of the United States, see my essay on *"Freedom and Democratic Socialism"* for an understanding of mixed economies. Many of us take capitalism for granted or have a microscopic understanding of its true nature. However, suppose capitalism is to be truly understood. In that case, one must acknowledge that man is a free, independent individual capable of making sound economic decisions within the bounds of every just restraint.[183] That includes the freedom to choose to starve if one so desires. This concept separates capitalism from all other economic systems and is why it is commonly known as the free enterprise or free market system.

> *"In a capitalist society, all human relationships are voluntary. Men are free to cooperate or not, to deal with one another or not, as their own individual judgments, convictions, and interests dictate. They can deal with one another only in terms of and by means of reason, i.e., by means of discussion, persuasion, and contractual agreement, by voluntary choice to mutual benefit."*[184]
> ~ Ayn Rand.

The terms Capitalism and capitalist were initially meant as a smear by Karl Marx. It was intended to imply a system run by the greedy to exploit the workers. Marx unintentionally gave great merit to a system that allows individuals to choose their occupations, sell their products at whatever prices they prefer, and select from among products to obtain the best value.[185] As noted in my essay on *"Freedom and Democratic Socialism,"* socialists cannot comprehend this freedom embedded within capitalism, nor can such freedom be maintained within a socialist economic model.

Capitalism is an economic system characterized by individual private ownership of production and property, organized around freedom, voluntary exchange, and pricing. According to Ayn Rand, a Russian-American novelist and philosopher, capitalism is defined as a social system that recognizes individual rights, including property rights, in which all property is privately owned.[186]

> *"Private property creates for the individual a sphere in which he is free of the state. It sets limits to the operation of the authoritarian will. It allows other forces to arise side by side with and in opposition to political power. It thus becomes the basis of all those activities that are free from violent interference on the part of the state. It is the soil in which the seeds of freedom are nurtured and in which the autonomy of the individual and ultimately all intellectual and material progress are rooted."* [187] ~Ludwig von Mises.

Private property, individual rights, and private ownership, which capitalism can only bring into complete existence, are the outward displays of freedom and individual thought and action. Socialism fails in so much as when everyone owns something, no one owns it, and no one has a direct interest in maintaining or improving its condition.[188] Private property and individual private ownership in general and as the means of production are the bedrock of individual, political, and economic freedom. To be secure in one's person and property dates back throughout history. For this reason, socialists want to destroy this superior purpose of liberty. Socialists believe that only a small subset of individuals in society, nearly always including themselves, have the wherewithal or knowledge of what to produce, how to produce it, and for whom it should be produced. This belief is, without a doubt, problematic, given no one person or set of individuals can hope to plan or organize an entire economic system of transactions.

Given capitalism is structured around freedom, your economic freedom of choice within a competitive economy rests on the fact that if a business refuses to satisfy your desire for a product, you can quickly pivot to another business that will. It is precisely because of such freedom of choice that enjoyment of effort or labor is done. The individual has the authority to direct all economic activity within their lives and to determine which economic tradeoffs must be made. Socialism removes that freedom to choose and one's authority to direct one's economic activity, replacing it with government authority, i.e., collective government selectivity of individual tradeoffs. While few people ever have an abundance of choice in all economic opportunities and situations, it is particularly imperative to note that some level of economic choice is still available. How unbearable would it be knowing no amount of effort you make can change the fact you must only choose the government-sanctioned loaf of bread or car to purchase?

Pricing and Price Controls

Given that capitalism is made up of voluntary exchanges between individuals, free to choose which products to purchase and whom to purchase those products from for mutual benefit, there must be a mechanism to communicate one's intent. Prices are that mechanism. While there are numerous economic theories of pricing, it is essential to remember that prices are the signals, undergirded by supply and demand, that communicate to each individual what to buy, what to produce, in what quantities, and what resources are scarce.

> *"Prices are important not because money is considered paramount but because prices are a fast and effective conveyor of information through a vast society in which fragmented knowledge must be coordinated."* ~ Thomas Sowell.

No one individual or set of individuals is responsible for coordinating economic activities or transactions in a capitalist economy. Each person is responsible for the pricing and purchasing within their sphere of influence. Their different pricing and purchases signal to others how much of each resource gets used, where, and how the resulting products get transferred to others. For example, an individual purchasing a pencil at the price of one dollar signals to the manufacturer that the person is willing to commit to voluntary exchange. Moreover, those purchases also signal to the manufacturer that their purchase of labor, lead, wood, and other scarce resources used to make the pencil were correctly purchased. Notwithstanding, each company the pencil manufacturer purchased raw materials and resources from, including labor, will be signaled simultaneously.

In a socialist economy, the decisions as to what to buy, what to produce, how much, and from whom are not guided by prices. Instead, a central planning board, government agency, or select individuals motivated by various political ideologies decide what to produce, how much, and from whom. Thus, it is this small group that performs the functions of the market, or signal communicator, which removes all freedom from the process. Moreover, when the government interferes with prices, i.e., price controls, it eliminates the ability of free people to make intelligent economic decisions.[189]

According to economist Thomas Sewell, price control laws date back as far as ancient Egypt and Babylon and have been imposed at one time or another on every continent. For thousands of years throughout history, the actual consequences of such price control laws have been on full display.[190] Price controls are typically a political response to economic price changes. More often than not, price controls are enacted to keep prices low after significant political pressure. The artificially low prices are generally excellent in the short run to gain political clout, but more significant economic damage is done over the long term. If effectively enforced, such legal or voluntary controls would eventually destroy the free-enterprise system and will be replaced by a centrally controlled system.[191]

> *"While price controls might save you some money…, they will cost you time and money in the form of shortages, long lines, and perhaps rationing because it will no longer be profitable for companies to deliver gas to your local gas station."*[192]

Venezuela is home to the world's largest oil reserves, yet the country continues to run out of gasoline. According to the newspaper El Nacional, one-third of Venezuela's 24 states – Miranda, Aragua, Lara, Barinas, Anzoátegui, Nueva Esparta, Bolívar, and Monagas, reported significant shortages in gasoline for sale in stations throughout these cities.[193] A Reuters investigation revealed that the current Venezuelan president's policy of exporting, often for very little or no profit, to countries who support Venezuela's socialist government has caused the 77 refineries to shut down.[194]

> *"Hundreds of Venezuelans found themselves stranded…as the nation's gasoline supply ran out at stations throughout the nation's urban centers."*[195]

Hugo Chavez introduced price controls on essential goods such as sugar, coffee, rice, milk, and flour, to name a few. These price controls were done to make basic goods affordable to the masses. A policy continued under the current Venezuelan president. These fixed prices led businesses to complain that the new price control rules were forcing them to produce these goods at a loss. Subsequently, the companies could not or refused to produce the goods for government-run stores or simply shut down altogether. Price controls enacted to make essential goods cheaper and score political points for the Venezuelan president created Venezuela's subsequent inflation of 2,068 percent and black markets for these essential goods, making said products more scarce and less affordable.

With businesses unwilling to produce products because of price controls, a shortage of goods was immediately seen with long wait lines for the few products left. Hoarding by citizens occurred, as well as black markets and cartel activities began to grip the markets, making it almost impossible to obtain the products. This hurt the citizens, so price controls were instituted to protect them.

Moreover, price controls quickly become a tool for the government to turn citizens against one another. Ralph R. Reiland reported in his 2007 Capitalism Magazine article on the Zimbabwean economic crisis that the price controls initiated by the Zimbabwean government only worsened the situation. To keep citizens in line, Zimbabwe's security forces were given the authority to observe citizens' e-mails and tap their phones. Business owners were threatened with jail and the nationalization of their companies if they did not obey pricing laws.

"Bread, sugar, and cornmeal, staples of every Zimbabwean's diet, have vanished, seized by mobs who denuded stores like locusts in

wheat fields. Meat is virtually nonexistent, even for members of the middle class who have money to buy it on the black market. Gasoline is nearly unobtainable. Hospital patients are dying for lack of basic medical supplies. Power blackouts and water cutoffs are endemic. As many as 4,000 businesspeople have been arrested, fined, or jailed while state-run newspapers publish lists of telephone numbers on their front pages daily, exhorting citizens to report merchants whose prices exceed the dictates."[196]

In March 2017, Venezuela authorities arrested four bakers in response to a national bread shortage. Venezuela National Superintendent for the Defense of Socioeconomic Rights charged the four bakers and temporarily seized their bakeries, accusing the bakers of being part of a broad 'economic war' aimed at destabilizing the country.[197] Their crime was illegally using price-regulated flour to make specialty items, like sweet rolls and croissants.[198]

It is also worth noting that all forms of price controls by any other name are still the same and that such controls do not lead to an increased availability of a product or human capital. That is to say, rent controls, minimum wage laws, etc., will all eventually result in the same outcome of closed stores, shortages, and hoarding. This is evidenced by the City of Seattle's $15 per hour minimum wage law. A study of the effects of the minimum wage law found that the new law did not assist some workers, given their pay would have likely increased with experience and tenure on the job. While other workers were earning more, fewer had jobs, and still others who did retain work worked fewer hours than they had without the minimum wage law. The study also noted the loss of small businesses or opportunities to work.[199]

Let's look at the example of lakefront property, which is quite a scarce resource. The higher price reflects and signals to others the supply, demand, and limited availability of that resource. Therefore, a price control scheme on such property will not make more property available; it would lead to hoarding by those lucky enough to purchase it. Moreover, under socialism or another equality scheme, there would still be scarcity and a lack of lakefront property no matter what social advocacy movement for equality was in fashion. Further, under socialism, there would be limited opportunities to own such a scarce resource, allowing for the apparent hypocrisy of socialist leaders to take advantage of the hoarding. For example, admitted socialist New York City Mayor Bill De Blasio often calls for further rent freezes on the city's more than one million rent-controlled apartments yet raises the rent on properties he owns.[200]

Fallacies of Capitalism

Now that you have a fundamental understanding of capitalism, prices, and the pitfalls of price controls, we can now examine the fallacies surrounding capitalism. A fallacy is a mistaken belief based on faulty reasoning, misleading or unsound argument or information. These fallacies are instead ingrained in an individual's system of beliefs based on one's pre-existing vision. As Thomas Sowell noted, the practice of not subjecting trendy beliefs to the test of facts but accepting or rejecting said beliefs according to how they fit into one's pre-existing vision is exceedingly problematic, if not dangerous.[201]

Initially, I believe it essential to review various basic economic fallacies. This examination will allow for a greater understanding of the larger fallacies of capitalism and a clearer idea of the economic truth of socialism. The first of these basic economic fallacies is the fallacy of collective terms. All respectable economists recognize that the only thinking and acting entity is the individual and that all human actions spawn from the individual. This is why terms such as "society," "community," "nation," "class," and "us." As it relates to economics, these are abstract constructs. The fallacy here is falsely assuming that the collective is, in fact, a thinking and acting entity on its own and is not made up of individuals. In reality, everything that occurs and its consequence originates in an identifiable individual.

For example, the collective term "family" would be hollow if all individuals were removed or disappeared. This fallacy of collective terms and generalizations is at the core backbone of socialism. While capitalism, as noted above, focuses on the individual, not the collective. Socialists will commonly use collective terms in discussions of inequality, assuming that wealth is a societal pie created by the society as a whole, which must be divided fairly. However, wealth is not created by society as a whole but produced by individuals. Therefore, for society to distribute any wealth under a misguided attempt at fairness, it must first seize such wealth from individuals.

Another of these basic economic fallacies is the fallacy of composition. This fallacy or error is similar to the first in so much that it involves individuals. However, it is the mistaken belief that what holds true for one individual will hold true for all others. For example, if a person stands up during a sporting event, obviously that person would see the event more clearly; however, if all attendees were to stand, the view of many people would be significantly worsened. Further, if a counterfeiter were to print a million dollars, were he not to be apprehended, would most certainly benefit.

Nevertheless, if all citizens were to have the ability to print money, inflation would most certainly skyrocket, creating havoc on the economy as a whole. Therefore, as we can clearly see, what might benefit one individual will not benefit all. Unfortunately, numerous governmental policies are based on this fallacy. Politicians enact legislation to aid one group, industry, or particular interest, claiming its net benefit to or in the best interest of all. Consequently, this and the aforementioned fallacy inevitably lead to distortions on freedom, as noted in my essay *"Freedom and Democratic Socialism."*

The fallacy of the Zero-Sum is another of the primary economic fallacies. This fallacy is the false assumption that all economic transactions are a zero-sum process, I.E., what one individual gains is lost by another individual. This false assumption is why most modern critics of capitalism fear economic freedom by virtue of this fallacy. They fear the results of allowing people the freedom to decide their economic affairs and letting the unregulated market run its course because of this fallacy handed down from generations of misinformation. This fallacy has given rise to the belief that regulators and bureaucrats know better than private citizens in making their voluntary arrangements, and therefore, regulators are needed to prevent individuals from suffering loss. Those who believe this fallacy fail to realize that economic transactions again are voluntary and that an individual would not, and is not, compelled to enter into a transaction without mutual acceptance. Moreover, suffering an economic loss is not a bad thing. It causes individuals and businesses to reorient and reallocate resources for better uses.

> *"Voluntary economic transaction, whether between employer and employee, tenant and landlord, or international trade would not continue to take place unless both parties were better off making these transactions than not making them."*[202]

The Zero-Sum fallacy also gives rise to the delusion that society has bestowed upon every man certain societal rights. According to this doctrine, society is openhanded toward every person born. There is plenty of everything for everybody despite the obvious scarcity. Consequently, it demands that every person has a claim against all their fellow men and against society as a whole, to which the individual is entitled to get the full portion of which society has allotted to them. In ignorance, The doctrine would argue that a poor individual is only poor because another unjust individual has stolen or deprived them of their right to be rich.[203] However, those who believe in such a fallacy fail to note the obvious questions that arise: who will determine what claims against society are valid, and or what is the exact portion an individual is entitled to have?

Fallacy: U.S. is a Pure Capitalist System

One of the biggest misconceptions perpetuated from generation to generation is the belief that the US is, in fact, a true free-market capitalist system. Moreover, I argue that on a scale of one to ten, ten being the best pure capitalism and one being the worst, pure socialism/communism-- the US has gone from a score of 8 to a score of 5, crony capitalism. That is to say, while there is a certain amount of capitalism left in the US markets, cronyism is just as prevalent and is overtaking the markets by those in power. It is also worth noting that this ranking is my personal ranking, based on my criteria. Likewise, a ranking from the Heritage Foundation 2016 Index of Economic Freedom report stated that the United States remains stalled in the ranks of the "mostly free," second-tier economic freedom status into which it dropped in 2010. The report also noted that America's vibrant entrepreneurial growth is significantly hampered by intrusive, expensive, and often ineffective government policies and that government favoritism toward deep-rooted interests has impaired innovation and contributed to a jaded recovery and stagnant income growth. The US economic freedom score has declined from 81.2, or number 5 in the world, in 2007 to 75.4, or number 11, in 2016.[204] The report contributes the sharp decline to the explosion in government spending, a dramatic rise in the national debt, the government takeover of healthcare, and the massive growth in government regulation and investment uncertainty.

This cronyism or unfair practice by which an individual of power provides favoritism to colleagues, family, or friends has created an environment of Crony capitalism in America. Crony capitalism is an economy in which success in transactions or business generally depends on close relationships and favoritism between a person of power and business people. It is exhibited by favoritism in the distribution of legal permits, government grants, special tax breaks, or other forms of state interventionism. It should be noted that the more cronyism you add to an economy, the more tyrannical the economy becomes.

Crony capitalism is very wasteful and distorts the broader economy at large. Industries such as healthcare, student loans, energy, and agriculture fall victim to politicized decisions that have wide-ranging and detrimental effects within the US markets. This Crony capitalism is evident with Solyndra, a California-based green energy solar panel manufacturer that received $535 million in stimulus-funded loan guarantees from the US Department of Energy. Soon after, the company filed for bankruptcy, leaving 1,100 people out of work and taxpayers obligated for the $535 million in federal loans. Matters were made worse when it was revealed that federal Office of Management and Budget officials felt pressured by the Obama administration to approve the loan despite an awareness of Solyndra's financial instability.[205] Additionally, obtained White House e-mails suggest that President Obama's original idea for involvement originated with his then Chief of Staff, Rahm Emanuel.[206]

> *"There are no necessary evils in government; Its evils exist only in its abuses."* ~ *President Andrew Jackson.*

While there are too many examples of crony capitalism to list within the confines of this essay, it is worth noting that socialists now have Americans accepting the crony capitalism and Marxist view that the government's economic class destination and redistribution is capitalism. The purpose of which is to distort economics and destroy the existence of private property rights and the possibility of true economic freedom. Further, given that any economic system with significant government controls is not capitalism and there is a large degree of cronyism within the US markets, the only real choice this would leave is the choice as to which degree of socialism individuals prefer. That is to say. The argument is no longer about freedom and free markets but about how much or how little the government should be involved in the market.

Fallacy: Capitalists Are Greedy and Create Envy

"Capitalism is relatively new in human history. Prior to capitalism, the way people amassed great wealth was by looting, plundering, and enslaving their fellow man. Capitalism made it possible to become wealthy by serving your fellow man."[207]

"Capitalists are greedy" is something I hear all too often in this modern era of the millennials and iPhones. A popular complaint is CEOs are greedy for their enormous salaries, or as gas prices rise, critics see that oil companies are greedy and want more profits. While the greedy argument against capitalism makes for a great bumper sticker, greed alone cannot obtain wealth. You could become so greedy that you want a fortune twice the size of Warren Buffet—but this greed would not increase your income by one cent.[208]

The underlying problem with the greedy argument against capitalism is that it makes no distinction between greed and self-interest within a capitalist system. Moreover, we are simply left to assume that powerful people in a capitalist system are all inherently evil, while influential people in socialist systems are somehow extremely benevolent. Capitalism, at its core, is a competition of giving to others. It channels an individual's self-interest into self-sacrifice. For example, entrepreneurs can only profit or help themselves by helping others achieve upward mobility.

Before I continue, it is important to note that greed and self-interest exist in all economic systems, whether capitalism or socialism. The problem occurs when critics of capitalism do not understand the difference between greed and self-interest or that greed is absent in a socialist economic model. Self-interest is about self-preservation, responsibility, and increased quality of life and is the motivation behind why one will go to work in the morning or seek education.[209] Greed is concerned with seeking all at the expense of others and is motivated not to assist others but to dominate others and to achieve to the detriment of others.

Socialists often assert moral superiority by claiming greed does not drive them or that they are somehow more magnanimous. However, given that greed is more concerned with seeking all at the expense of others, is it not greedy to want free college and accessible healthcare and make others provide and pay for such services? Socialism produces people whose preoccupations become increasingly selfish, i.e., how many benefits will I receive? Will the government pay for my tuition? Will the government pay for health care?[210]

> *"Whatever its intentions, socialism produces far more selfish individuals and a far more selfish society than a free-market economy does. And once this widespread selfishness catches on, it is almost impossible to undo it."*[211]

Furthermore, socialists claim to dislike capitalism and excess wealth unless they are the beneficiaries of such capitalism. For example, Bernie Sanders, an admitted socialist, purchased a beachfront vacation home worth nearly $600,000. This is his third home.[212] According to the US Census Bureau, only 63.5% of Americans own a single home[213] and even fewer own multiple homes. Would it not then be greedy to own multiple residences when so few can only afford to own one?

The economic fallacy of capitalist greed also breeds within some individuals an overwhelming need to try and pursue socialism within their sphere of business influence. This pursuit is commonly done by those so as not to appear greedy, thereby creating a false sense of righteousness. This strong desire to not appear greedy and look benevolent is an egocentric socialistic intent that has led to subpar business models and monumental business failures. For example, the Garden Diner and Cafe in Grand Rapids, Michigan, featured a vegan, vegetarian, and raw food menu that was met with significant national acclaim. The owners' socialistic business model did not allow for bosses or managers; they promised a high 'living wage' to all employees and obtained strong union participation.[214] Ongoing customers complained of waiting more than 40 minutes for a single sandwich. The restaurant's equal pay and no tipping scheme failed to reward exceptional service, and sporadic restaurant hours of operation, given hours that were voted on by the employees, frequently leaving the restaurant closed, contributed to the inevitable restaurant's demise.

Moreover, customers noted on the restaurant's message board that *"you shouldn't try running your business on political goodwill alone."*[215] More or less implying that there is some level of self-interest that must be aspired to. Consequently, the restaurant could not make enough profit to stay afloat, and the owner's benevolent socialistic intent to be fair and not appear greedy created an equality of unemployment and insufficiency for all former employees.

In another example, the state of California, in an effort to appear magnanimous toward people with low incomes, enacted a rise in the minimum wage to be phased in over time, with the ultimate goal of $15 per hour by 2021. After two years in business, a small clothing manufacturer was forced to relocate to Las Vegas in an effort to remain open. The company, with more than 150 clients and 18 employees, would stand to lose in excess of $200,000 a year and far more once the workforce grows after the $15 minimum wage is fully phased in.[216] Similarly, the socialistic Venezuela government has announced a 50% increase in the country's monthly minimum wage and pensions, which is the fifth increase in less than a year, to combat the 2,068 percent inflation. This minimum wage amounts to 40,000 bolivars, about $60. Business leaders believe the wage increase could result in layoffs and force the remaining small businesses to close.[217]

Let's turn the focus to envy and the question, Does capitalism breed envy? This question and the envy fallacy assume that envy is not present in any other economic system or that envy only exists because of capitalism. Envy has existed from the foundation of time and is older than any economic system or political ideology. Envy is present in capitalistic and socialistic economies. However, capitalism transforms envy into aspiration and admiration through freedom of voluntary exchange. Under socialism, envy is not required to transform and would subsequently manifest as theft. Socialism uses envy to fuel resentment as it seeks justice through redistribution or legalized theft.

In a capitalist society that rewards initiative and offers many opportunists, such a free market will foster innovation, aspiration, and ambition. In socialist societies with significantly less economic freedom, you find high levels of envy and resentment. Such envy is the case in socialist countries, where people continue to demand more government benefits rather than to keep more of what they have earned.

> *"And since 1973, the General Social Survey has asked Americans this question: Some people say that people get ahead by their hard work; others say that lucky breaks or help from other people are more important. Which do you think is most important? For 40 years, between 60 percent and 70 percent of Americans have chosen hard work. "*[218]

In a recent poll, the Pew Research Center found that 88 percent of Americans admired citizens who get rich by working hard.[219] The World Values Survey conducted between 2005 and 2007 asked people in 54 nations whether or not success is a byproduct of hard work or luck and connections. Americans were found to be more likely than people in other countries, and twice as likely as the French, to say success comes from hard work.[220]

Americans, as a whole, are not envious. A select few thrust the movement of envy to appear magnanimous and push for socialistic change around a redistribution of individual wealth. One can always find an individual who harbors resentment against pale abstractions such as "management," "capital," and or "Wall Street." But, those ideas or faint shadows are more apparent and magnified within the socialist economic system, not a capitalist one.[221]

Fallacy: Capitalism Increases Poverty

This misconception that capitalism increases poverty is predicated on the ignorance of individuals to distinguish between poverty and inequality. The mistaken belief that those obtaining success under capitalism should be obligated to support those in poverty, given that capitalism created such poverty in the first place. This false narrative assumes several factors in error. The first such erroneous belief has the Zero-Sum Fallacy at its core. To adhere to the delusion that capitalism increases poverty, one has to believe that those who are thriving under capitalism gain such success from stealing or cheating others, namely those who are in poverty.

Consequently, this fosters the false narrative that equality must now be obtained and that the government is the sole benevolent force that can assist in combating such poverty. The mistaken belief that the government knows how best to redistribute resources in the fairest manner. I contend that trusting a government of self-interested people to know how to redistribute individual wealth ethically is naïve, ignorant, and reckless.[222] It should also be noted that I do not believe that the government bears a responsibility to low-income people, as some would suggest. This statement is based mainly on the fallacy of collective terms undergirded with pure socialistic intent. If they so choose, individuals bear responsibility for people with low incomes.[223] The fact that economic opportunities open to people experiencing poverty in a free market may be more restricted than those open to others does not make it less accurate that in such a free market, people experiencing poverty are much more accessible and economically advantaged than those demanding greater material comfort in a socialist economy.[224] Moreover, in the United States, the majority of our citizens today have never experienced genuine abject poverty and are the wealthiest "poor" in the world.

Critics of capitalism hold an arrogant view of their ability to be benevolent, which gives rise to a false belief that poverty in the US is similar to poverty in other countries and that capitalism causes such poverty. Therefore, it is pertinent to define poverty in the US, or the poverty line as economists know it. The U.S. Census Bureau defines poverty as anyone with an annual income of less than $24,036 or $65 a day. For a family of four, this amounts to $15 per day per person for food, clothing, housing, medical care, transportation, and education. The Census Bureau estimates that as of 2015,

13.5% of the U.S. population lives in poverty per this definition.[225]

However, the U.S. Census Bureau's definition of poverty is rarely used by anyone other than economists or political scientists. Socialists believe poverty in the US to be children with insects buzzing around their faces and wearing tattered clothing. This is simply not the case. As defined by the US government, the typical poor household has a car, two color televisions, cable or satellite TV, a DVD player, air conditioning, and a VCR. If there are children, especially boys, the family has a game system, such as an Xbox or PlayStation.[226]

This high standard of living for the US poor is unheard of worldwide. Conversely, it is again necessary for me to define, concisely the poverty line for people living outside the US. Most economists subscribe to the thought that $1 a day is the line by which to measure extreme poverty, while the World Bank redefined extreme poverty as $1.90 per day in 2015. Some economists use numbers ranging from $3.10 per day to as much as $15 per day. I have chosen to use $1.00 per day as the definition of extreme poverty as I examine the data unless otherwise noted.

In 1820, the vast majority of people living in the world were living in extreme poverty, with only a tiny elite enjoying higher standards of living. Estimates suggest anywhere between 84 to 94 percent lived in extreme poverty.[227] Poverty worldwide declined from 94 percent in 1820 to 17 percent in

2011.[228] The World Bank estimates global poverty declined from 44 percent in 1980 to 10 percent in 2015.[229]

While global poverty rates are decreasing overall, I think it prudent to offer further clarity by reviewing two distinct countries that have used different economic systems to fight poverty. As noted in my essay *"Freedom and Democratic Socialism,"* Venezuela is a country ravaged by socialism. The mantra of egalitarianism to combat poverty has only proven to foster equal impoverishment. My review of World Bank data found that the Venezuela poverty rate, based on $1.90 per day, has furcated wildly from 55.6 percent in 1997 to 33.1 percent in 2015.[230] Socialism has utterly failed to reduce poverty for those Venezuelans living on $1.90 a day, below one-third or 33 percent. It should also be noted that this World Bank data does not consider the current economic failures of the socialist Venezuelan government.

In contrast, China, which shifted from a centrally-planned economy (socialism) to a free market-based economy (capitalism) in 1978, has steadily decreased poverty from 42.5 percent in 1996 to 1.85 percent in 2013.[231] Overall, China has reduced poverty significantly using free market-based reforms. It went from an estimated poverty rate of 88.32 percent in 1981 to an estimated poverty rate of 1.85 percent in 2013.[232] That means China has gone from 88.32 percent of its population living on just $1.90 a day to just 1.85 percent of its population living on $1.90 a day in just under 40 years due to capitalism.

Between 1999 and 2016, the average per capita income in Venezuela rose by only 2 percent, while in the rest of Latin America and the Caribbean, the average per capita income increased by 41 percent.[233] Similar income issues took place in another socialist economy, Zimbabwe. Income per person of Zimbabwean citizens declined by 25 percent, while Africa's income per person rose by 48 percent.[234]

If we examine the economies of North Korea, a socialist dictatorship, and South Korea, a capitalist democracy, we can see stark differences. Comparing a clear fundamental example of the differences between socialism and capitalism. Both countries are located in the same geographic regions. Both have similar natural resources and similar ethnic population makeup. However, North Korea, under socialism, has continued to heavily regulate the economy through central planning and control, where entrepreneurship is virtually impossible, all property belongs to the government, and the government determines wages and employment.[235] According to the Heritage Foundation, North Korea's Gross Domestic Product (GDP) is a mere 17.4 billion, with zero economic growth.

Further, given its meager GDP, the North Korean government routinely warns its population of impending food shortages and starvation. *"The state-run Rodong Sinmun reminded all North Koreans they must be willing to die for dictator Kim Jong-un if necessary."*[236] South Korea's daily news reported that in 2016, North Korea needed to import an estimated 440,000 tons of food to feed its inhabitants, yet it has only been able to purchase 17,600 tons. The paper also reported that the North Korean government now requires its citizens to give back one kilogram of rice every month.[237]

In contrast, South Korea's GDP is 1.8 trillion dollars, with an economic growth rate of 2.6 percent. South Koreans enjoy property rights, a competitive regulatory framework facilitating entrepreneurial activity and innovation, a dynamic labor market, and an abundant food supply.[238] It is apparent that the massive economic gap between North and South Korea is a clear reflection of the failure of North Korea's socialistic centrally planned economy.

> *"Perhaps the most critical lesson for today's tumultuous times is that the proven superiority of the free-market system and the value of economic liberty must be steadfastly reiterated."*[239]

These examples and World Bank data unmistakably indicate that only a free market economy can raise the standard of living for those in poverty. Moreover, free-market capitalism has done more to eradicate poverty throughout history than any other economic system. Consequently, capitalism does not increase poverty; it eradicates it.

Conclusion

Every socialist hopes to continue to promote a progressive socialist democracy that neutralizes capitalism and facilitates some form of real utopia. From this essay, you can unmistakably see the delusional fallacy of that hope. The demonstrated dominance of capitalism to eradicate poverty and use greed to benefit all reveals that those rejecting capitalism on moral grounds as an unfair system are genuinely misguided by their failure to comprehend what capitalism is and what benefits capitalism holds. Therefore, if capitalism is to be truly understood, one must acknowledge the concept that man is a free, independent individual capable of making sound economic decisions within the bounds of every just restraint.[240] However, as long as people are free to make such economic decisions, some will earn more than others, and some will have more than others. Socialism seeks equality for a so-called greater moral good and tries to be all things to everyone. However, the only actual verified accomplishment of socialism is that it has made most people equal in poverty and a choice few wealthy.

Chapter 4

SECOND AMENDMENT
AND GUN CONTROL

"To conquer a nation, first disarm its citizens." ~ Adolf Hitler.

JEAN-LUC, I WITNESSED A gentleman proudly displaying his "Second Amendment" tee shirt as he entered a store that exhibited a "Gun Free Zone" sign. While I calmly walked beside him, a female patron gave some angry, unsolicited words as she exited. She stated, *"Your shirt offends me, and I hope President Obama passes strict gun control...the blood of the innocent is on yours and the NRA's hands for the gun culture in America."* The utter ridiculousness of this statement and the apparent anti-intellectualism of the patron overshadowed her poorly conceived message. First, the woman exhibited an erroneous understanding of the core government's three-branch structure, I.E., a US president cannot pass legislation; it is the job of Congress, and two, believing that the NRA is physically killing anyone. Nevertheless, she was correct on one point. There is a gun culture in America, and as we explore the topic of the Second Amendment and, by extension, gun control in this essay, it will become abundantly clear that such a culture is very much a good thing.

From witnessing the encounter, it is apparent that merely displaying or uttering the words 'second amendment' will trigger some and cause others to shutter and panic. This encounter sparked a question in my mind about the Second Amendment and gun control in general. This essay will examine the subject of the second amendment and gun control. However, before I do, I believe it is initially necessary to explore the concepts and construction of the Second Amendment briefly. Then, I will review the subject of gun control and deconstruct some of the fallacies asserted by opponents of the Second Amendment. It should also be noted that this essay is not an exhaustive review of the Second Amendment or gun control issues, nor should it be viewed as such. What follows is my humble understanding of the issue.

Second Amendment

To accomplish an essential understanding of the Second Amendment argument raging within the modern era, you must first seek to understand the text of the Constitution and its origin.

> *"A well-regulated Militia, being necessary to the security of a free State, the right of the people to keep and bear Arms, shall not be infringed."*[241]

This surprisingly simple passage has produced controversy among supporters and opponents alike. The words "militia," 'right of the people' and 'keep and bear arms' are all being decidedly questioned and debated in this modern era. Second Amendment supporters affirm the right to keep and bear arms is an individual right, much like the freedom of speech, while opponents believe that the right to keep and bear arms are not individual and it pertains only to memberships in collective bodies, i.e., the military, police, or National Guard.[242] Opponents, believing that the Constitution does not afford any individual an absolute right to own a firearm, cling to the fallacy of collective terms, as described in my essay *"Capitalism and Morality,"* to justify their distortions on freedom.[243] As you will see later in this essay, this "collective" theory of interpreting the Second Amendment is nothing more than the redistribution of gun ownership to a select few and relies heavily on the government for collective safety.

When examining the origin of the Second Amendment, it is necessary to probe the original authors' and framers' intent when they authored the text. It is imperative to consider the original context of the true application of this amendment, given the collective theory of interpreting and the legal pretext for removing freedom. Thomas Jefferson cautioned Supreme Court Justice William Johnson that every question of construction concerning the Constitution should be viewed in light of when the Constitution was adopted.[244] James Wilson, an original Justice of the Supreme Court, also gave a comparable warning: to interpret the Constitution, one must discover the meaning of those who wrote it.[245] It is well defined from archives, writings, and established legal commentaries surrounding the Constitution from that period that the authors, framers, and other legal scholars of that day believed in the natural right of self-defense.

> *"Supreme Being gave existence to man, together with the means of preserving and beautifying that existence. He ... invested him [man] with an inviolable right to personal liberty and personal safety."[246] ~ Alexander Hamilton.*

> *"The ... right of the [citizens] that I shall at present mention is that of having arms for their defense. ... [Which is] the natural right of resistance and self-preservation."[247] ~ William Blackstone.*

> *"[Self]-defense, or self-preservation, is one of the first laws of nature, which no man ever resigned upon entering into society."[248] ~ Zephaniah Swift.*

Furthermore, it was also evident from literature and legal commentaries that the framers and other legal scholars from that period distinctly understood that the natural right of self-defense was an inalienable individual right and that the Second Amendment merely documented that right. Such was done to ensure that each citizen would retain that right in the face of the government's continual hunger to restrict freedom.

> *"The right of self-defense is the first law of nature: in most governments, it has been the study of rulers to confine this right within the narrowest limits possible. Wherever ... the right of the*

people to keep and bear arms is, under any color or pretext whatsoever, prohibited, liberty, if not already annihilated, is on the brink of destruction. "[249]

"The right of a citizen to bear arms, in lawful defense of himself or the State, is absolute. He does not derive it from the State government. It is one of the high powers delegated directly to the citizen and 'is excepted out of the general powers of government.' A law cannot be passed to infringe upon or impair it because it is above the law and independent of the lawmaking power. "[250]

Some framers dreaded a professional standing army and feared an invasion from other countries. Moreover, given the explicit right of individual self-defense that was ingrained into the newly minted Americans, the Second Amendment was therefore written to guarantee the right of citizens to arm themselves and join militias. The Second Amendment recognized and documented decades of tradition into one single point of structured law.

Over the years, opponents of the Second Amendment have used the militia preface in that amendment to deliberately misinterpret and imply that the framers intended citizens to be armed only in the context of, or participation in, a standing militia under the state's authority.[251] This is, in fact, not the case. The word militia is part of the operative clause, which is the lead-in that announces a purpose and, in this context, was meant to reference all non-disabled male citizens 18-45 according to the Militia Act of 1792. Samuel Adams stated in writings to James Warren that a Militia is composed of free citizens or all citizens.[252] George Mason answered the question of who the militia was by replying that the militia consisted of all people.[253] The clear affirmation or proclamation here is that the framers envision a militia as all citizens or individuals, not just a specific population subset.

> *"We find that the history of the Second Amendment reinforces the plain meaning of its text, namely that it protects individual Americans in their right to keep and bear arms whether or not they are a member of a select militia or performing active military service or training. We reject the collective rights and sophisticated collective rights models for interpreting the Second Amendment."*[254]

An individual has the right to keep and bear arms, apart from joining a selected subset of the population. In this modern era, courts have also upheld this individual right. In 2001, the Emerson case in Texas was heard in a federal district court, which ruled that the right to bear arms was an individual right, and one did not have to belong to a militia or collective to exercise that right.[255] Likewise, as late as 2008, in the D.C. v Heller case, the Supreme Court, in a 5-4 decision, reaffirmed that the Second Amendment applied to individual rights, laying waste to the collective theory of militia in the Second Amendment.[256] A clear majority of Americans unmistakably agree with the ruling of the Supreme Court. After the D.C. v Heller case decision, Americans were asked if they believe the Second Amendment guarantees the rights of individual Americans to own guns, and 73% said yes.

Moreover, 7 out of 10 Americans are opposed to any law that would make the possession of a handgun illegal.[257]

> *"Congress shall make no law respecting an establishment of religion, or prohibiting the free exercise thereof, or abridging the freedom of speech, or of the press; or the right of the people peaceably to assemble, and to petition the Government for a redress of grievances."*[258]

It should also be noted that while these legal decisions are correct, based on the before-mentioned reasoning, the collective theory of interpretation heaped upon the second amendment suffers from a rather significant and glaring inconsistency and hypocrisy. Opponents of the individual right to keep and bear arms will lean on the word militia aspects of the Second Amendment as a crutch to push a socialist collective theory that only a select group, I.E., police and military, should own or use firearms. However, those same opponents will easily regurgitate the First Amendment, *"the right of the people peaceably to assemble"* and claim an individual right to free speech and assembly, negating the apparent fact that the word 'people' has the same meaning in both amendments.

> *"...it has been suggested that the Second Amendment protects the "collective" right of states to maintain militias, while it does not protect the right of "the people" to keep and bear arms... The phrase "the people" meant the same thing in the Second Amendment as it did in the First, Fourth, Ninth, and Tenth Amendments – that is, each and every free person..."*[259]

Gregory E. Parker

Gun Control

"The laws that forbid the carrying of arms, disarm only those who are neither inclined nor determined to commit crimes."[260] ~ *Cesare Beccaria.*

Now that we have taken a cursory examination of the Second Amendment, we will focus on gun control and some myths surrounding this issue. I believe it is prudent first to define what gun control is. Gun control is defined as the laws or established policies that regulate or restrict the manufacture, sale, transfer, possession, or use of firearms by individual citizens. The New York Times defined gun control as *"a broad term that covers any sort of restriction on what kinds of firearms can be sold and bought, who can possess or sell them, where and how they can be stored or carried, what duties a seller has to vet a buyer, and what obligations both the buyer and the seller have to report transactions to the government."*[261] I consider gun control and its accompanying laws to be thinly veiled attempts to socialize the individual right of self-defense and to place such self-defense in the hands of the government's collective security.

Let me explain: gun control advocates pursue an agenda of distortion on individual freedom through reduction by seeking the elimination of all firearms, declaring public safety will be enhanced. They perpetuate the theory that the government can provide for an individual's safety better than the individual or that the individual freedom of self-defense is somehow subservient to a criminal's individual right to due process. For example, Justin Curmi, writing for the Huffington Post, argued that Americans have no legal right to shoot a violent attacker because it violates the criminal's right to a fair trial. He stated, *"The main problem with the notion of self-defense is it imposes on justice, for everyone has the right for a fair trial. Therefore, using a firearm to defend oneself is not legal because if the attacker is killed, he or she is devoid of his or her rights."*[262] A similar sentiment was echoed by Temia Hariston, the mother of a black robbery suspect who died from a gunshot wound he suffered while robbing a Pizza Hut. She stated during an interview with CBS News that she believed the employee who shot her son had no right to do so and should have let the police handle the situation. *"If there was to be a death, it was not the place of the employee at Pizza Hut. That is the place of law enforcement. It was an act of desperation, but I do not believe that Michael would have hurt anyone. Why in the hell did this guy have a gun?"*[263] The robbery suspects fathers stated, *"Even a criminal has a right to a degree,"*[264] Likewise, ten democrat Nevada state Senators filed a bill to water down the current castle doctrine protections, effectively allowing criminals to take legal action against their victims if the victim fights back and injures the attacker. Under the proposed legislation, a rapist who breaks into a woman's home would be allowed to sue the woman if she interferes and injures the attacker. Similarly, a father who defends his family during a violent home invasion could be sued by the attackers.[265]

Essentially, the criminal's freedom to do as they desire supersedes another's freedom to be safe from harm. As we have seen in my essay "Freedom and Democratic Socialism," an individual will choose collective safety and security over freedom unless that safety is best obtained through their personal liberty. For instance, most Americans believe and acknowledge that a police force (collective safety and security) is necessary for civil society and are willing to relinquish some freedoms for such collective safety. However, most Americans agree that personal protection (individual safety) is also needed, and it is up to the individual to choose which protection method best suits them. A Gallup poll finds that among those who own firearms, personal safety/protection is most often cited as the reason for ownership, 60 percent, followed by hunting at 36 percent.[266]

In recent memory, the government has continually failed in the arena of collective safety, i.e., terrorist attacks, school shootings, illegal immigrants killing Americans, and the increased murder rates in cities with high levels of gun control. Further, government agencies have been known to misplace firearms entrusted to them and allow them to end up in the hands of criminals. The Immigration and Naturalization Service (INS) misplaced 539 weapons, including a gas-grenade launcher and 39 automatic rifles or machine guns, six of which were eventually linked to crimes, two were seized during arrests, and one was held as evidence in a homicide.[267] Moreover, In 2001, it was reported that the FBI lost 449 weapons, including machine guns.[268] These events only increase the momentum for individual freedom of protection through firearms.

Federal background checks, as well as local concealed handgun permits, increase following all mass shootings.[269] Since 2007, concealed handgun permits have increased 215 percent to more than 14.5 million. A record 1.7 million additional permits were issued between 2014 and 2015 alone.[270] In eight states where data is listed by gender, since 2012, the number of permits has increased by 161% for women and 85% for men.[271] While this may not be the most accurate way to determine gun sales, given that federal law prohibits keeping a national registry of all guns and their owners, it does, however, reveal a correlation and trend relative to the fact that Americans, when faced with government collective safety failures, hunger for individual freedom of self-defense. This individual freedom of self-defense, as opposed to the government's collective security, has even begun to infiltrate what are commonly known as socialist groups. After the Orlando mass shooting, in which a Muslim gunman opened fire, killing 50 people and injuring 50 more, the gay community soon after encouraged gay individuals to purchase firearms, stating, *"...the government is not able to keep you safe."*[272] A group, the Pink Pistols, was created in response to an article by Jonathan Rauch, a Brookings Institution senior fellow, who advocated lesbians and gays carry concealed weapons to protect themselves. Jonathan Rauch stated in that article, *"Being able to rely on ourselves for self-defense is an important part of standing up for ourselves."*[273] The group's membership tripled in size after the Orlando massacre.

In Paris, where stringent restrictions on firearm possession by average civilians are imposed, and even police officers are unarmed, mass shootings still occur. Owning a firearm in France for self-defense is essentially out of the question for average citizens. Notwithstanding, fully automatic AK-47s, which were apparently used by terrorists in the most recent attack in Paris, can be purchased or sold on the black market for less than $1,200 US dollars.[274] In the wake of the latest terrorist attacks in France, police are now demanding to be allowed to carry service firearms again. The trade unions representing municipal police are demanding that all police officers routinely carry a firearm. Christophe Leveillé, General Secretary of the FO Trade Union, stated: *"Our colleagues are unarmed and in danger, and something must be done."*[275] Deputy General Secretary Frantz Michel added, *"French people are being told that the government is doing everything it can to keep them safe, which is false."*[276]

As I have stated previously in this essay, gun control is an attempt to socialize the right of self-defense and to place such self-defense in the hands of the government's collective security. This socialist construct of self-defense does not stop at just guns. Amid the government's collective security failures against terrorism in Sweden, Swedes have taken to wearing body armor and bulletproof vests. Allan Widman, chairman of the Swedish parliamentary defense committee, now demands that Swedes should be prohibited from obtaining bulletproof vests to protect themselves from the increasing violence. He stated, *"I believe that the sense of personal security that wearing armor gives helps to lower the threshold for the use of serious violence."*[277] Moreover, given that vests are classified as military equipment in Sweden, the bill he has filed would make it illegal and punishable for individual citizens to wear body armor in public places.[278] Essentially leaving the right of self-defense in his country to the government collective, which is evidently not up to the task.

It is also interesting to note that gun control advocates do not appear to indeed be against guns, considering such advocates will obviously need the police to have guns to disarm the people. For example, gun control advocates strive for only the police or military to have access to firearms. That is not gun control; it is merely centralization of gun ownership in the hands of the government and the political elite. As evidenced by the California state legislature, in 2011, it sought to exempt itself from California concealed firearms law's "Good Cause" requirement. Bill SB 610 would have exempted members of Congress, California statewide elected officials, and members of the California legislature from said cause requirement *"for protection or self-defense,"* the bill noted. That section was removed prior to the bill's passage. In another example, Former California Democratic State Senator and candidate for California Secretary of State, Leland Yee, a staunch gun control advocate, was sentenced to five years in prison for accepting bribes and trafficking weapons. As a state

Senator, Yee strongly supported strict gun control laws and was named to the Brady Campaign's Gun Violence Prevention Honor Roll.[279]

> *"Yee's actions...vile...and the arms dealings particularly hypocritical given the politician's history of gun control advocacy."*[280] ~ *Yanan Wang.*

While promoting his latest Jason Bourne motion picture in Australia, Matt Damon proclaimed that he wished America would pass a gun ban similar to Australia. Lena Dunham, the actress, preceded to advocate for removing all guns from subway ads promoting the new movie Jason Bourne.[281] Matt Damon's hypocritical answer was, in effect, to do it to everyone else, just not to me. *"I totally get it, I mean, especially given what's going on recently, and I get not wanting to see a picture of a gun right now, and I don't blame her at all. I mean for marketing purposes of 'Jason Bourne' — I mean, he is a guy who runs around with a gun, so it's not gratuitous marketing, but certainly, in light of recent events I understand that impulse to tear the gun out of the picture."*[282]

As you can undoubtedly see from these examples, gun control, like any other socialist construct, only reduces freedom, creates black markets, and hurts the very people it was intended to help. Further, most gun control advocates pushing for gun confiscation or outright bans want those gun bans to apply to everyone else but themselves. This is highlighted by California lawmakers' belief that they alone are worthy of individual personal protection, while other California citizens must wait until the police arrive. According to the Department of Justice, as of 2013, the average police response time is 11 minutes.

Gun Control and Discrimination

"... I must say this concerning the great controversy over rifles and shotguns. The only thing I've ever said is that in areas where the government has proven itself either unwilling or unable to defend the lives and the property of Negroes, it's time for Negroes to defend themselves. Article number two of the constitutional amendments provides you and me the right to own a rifle or a shotgun. It is constitutionally legal to own a shotgun or a rifle." [283]
~ Malcolm X.

History provides convincing evidence that racism is at the core of gun control laws. Over and over again throughout American history, gun control was openly stated as a method for keeping free or enslaved blacks from obtaining firearms. Laws in the original colony of Virginia in 1640 declared enslaved people, and free blacks were barred from owning firearms. The Act for the Better Ordering of Negroes and Slaves, enacted by South Carolina in 1712, included significant no firearms provisions for blacks. [284]

After the Civil War, night riders, or Ku Klux Klan (KKK) groups, were created by Democrats in late 1865 to generate the correct level of terror in black victims. [285] The passage of the 14th Amendment by Republicans, while intended to offer protection for blacks from the Democrat's KKK raids, did not stop such intimidation or racist gun control laws as planned. Gun control shifted from outright bans to discretionary permitting. Discretionary permitting allows local law enforcement to determine who is suitable to carry a firearm. Some states and local governments required blacks to obtain permits, requiring hefty licensing fees, thereby allowing local police or licensing boards to keep whom they deemed "undesirable" from legally accessing firearms.[286] These requirements were done to make it significantly more difficult for blacks to defend themselves against night riders or KKK lynch mobs. Even Dr. Martin Luther King Jr, a southern preacher in the mid-1950s, applied for a concealed carry permit in Alabama after the firebombing of his home in 1956. The local police, using discretionary licensing policies, denied Dr. King a permit, claiming he was unsuitable.[287]

Clear evidence concerning this racist intent of gun control permitting laws can be found in the 1941 Florida Supreme Court case of Watson v. Stone involving a gun violation under an 1893 Act. Justice Buford wrote

> "The original Act of 1893 was passed when there was a great influx of negro laborers in this State drawn here for the purpose of working in turpentine and lumber camps. The same condition existed when the Act was amended in 1901, and the Act was passed for the purpose of disarming the negro laborers and to thereby reduce the unlawful homicides that were prevalent in turpentine and saw-mill camps and to give the white citizens in sparsely settled areas a better feeling of security. The statute was

never intended to be applied to the white population and in practice has never been so applied."[288]

Now the question becomes, has the modern era changed these discriminatory tactics? According to a 1986 Assembly Office of Research report, in liberal California, a discretionary "may issue" firearms permit state, where the police chiefs or sheriffs have complete discretion in granting an applicant a license, most permits are issued to white males. The report stated, *"In most cases, the permit holder is personally known to the local sheriff or chief of police...[with] the overwhelming majority of permit holders are white males."*[289] In Los Angeles County, California, with some 7.6 million people out of the state's 39+ million, there were only 173 permits issued as of 2013 and only 59,808 permits issued statewide.[290]

In the liberal State of Illinois, another discretionary 'may issue' firearms permit state, where the state police and county sheriffs have total discretion in granting an applicant a permit, as of 2014, only 73,714 permits were issued statewide. Only 8 percent had been issued to blacks, while 90 percent were issued to whites.[291] An examination at a county level, I.E., Cook County, where Chicago is located, shows a glaring disparity. The suburbs, which have a lower overall crime rate, comprised of 96 percent white residents with average incomes of $121,000, have a higher rate of registered concealed carry permit holders. In contrast to the south, Chicago, with an overall high crime rate and the most violent neighborhoods, comprised of 98 percent black residents with average incomes of $48,000, has significantly lower rates of registered

concealed carry permit holders. The 2014 article confirmed
that the crime-ridden neighborhoods of Chicago's Englewood,
West Englewood, and West Garfield Park have only 193
concealed carry license holders out of a total population of
114,933.[292]

> *"In these gangbang neighborhoods, people can't afford the license.
> They're making choices between food and medicine, and they can't
> even guarantee they'll get even that. We need to arm ourselves and
> protect ourselves from these gangbangers, but we just can't afford
> to do it."*[293]

In Illinois, a concealed carry license can cost as much as
$600, which does not include the firearms training cost at a
state-approved range. Moreover, given there are no gun
ranges in Chicago, the cost is significantly increased for low-
income citizens.

Proponents of gun control continue to make it difficult for
minorities to obtain firearms. Chicago Democrat Rep. Luis
Gutierrez continually authors legislation to ban the
production of inexpensive guns useful for self-defense.[294]
These firearms are the preferred choice of poorer potential
victims who cannot afford more expensive guns. Moreover, In
2013, the Obama administration lobbied the Colorado state
legislature to pass a bill that would impose both a tax and a
background check on the private transfers of all guns.[295]
Again, these background checks would disproportionately
affect the lower-income population adversely. In 2013,
Maryland Democrats passed legislation requiring the

licensing and registration of handguns, which can cost upwards of $230. Maryland Republicans tried to exempt poor individuals from paying government fees, but the Democrat-controlled state legislature did not allow the amendment to come up for a vote.[296]

Not only is gun control discriminatory, but it is also hypocritical. Let's look back to the case of Temia Hariston, the mother of a black robbery suspect who died from a gunshot wound he suffered while robbing a Pizza Hut. We can see the hypocrisy of identity politics within her comments.

> *"If there was to be a death, it was not the place of the employee at Pizza Hut. That is the place of law enforcement. It was an act of desperation, but I do not believe that Michael would have hurt anyone. Why in the hell did this guy have a gun?"*[297]

It is evident from her comments she believed that only the police should be allowed to use deadly force, *"If there was to be a death, it was not the place of the employee at Pizza Hut. That is the place of law enforcement."* This comment epitomizes the conflicts between identity groups that delegitimize the scope and activism of each group. Mrs. Hariston's statement that only the police should have used deadly force for her black son is in direct contradiction to the Black Lives Matter (BLM) advocacy, which believes all police officers are racist and should not be allowed to use deadly force against blacks. Further, BLM believes the police are the *"new slave catchers and are only out to kill blacks."*[298]

It is undoubtedly evident that gun control in the United States is based on a history of racism and discrimination by liberals. It is also apparent that liberals currently have, and appear to continue, to lead minorities toward the socialism of self-defense.

Gun-Free Zones Are Not the Answer

"No matter how many speeches a politician gives in favor of gun control, it's a safe bet that his own bodyguards are still packing heat. Even if he's giving a speech at a school or, post office, or other gun-free zone. The Secret Service and other professional bodyguard types apparently don't trust the ability of 'No guns allowed' signs to keep shooters from hitting their targets. That's the difference between public servants and the public they serve."[299]

The notion that criminals who refuse to comply with other laws would in some way obey gun-control laws or 'Gun Free Zone' signs is the height of asinine. Given this notion, proponents of gun control accept as true that citizens cannot be trusted to do the right thing with firearms, so they push laws against guns, which most law-abiding citizens will abide by because citizens can be trusted. This circular logic is on full display as US Representative Hank Johnson (D-Ga) reintroduced his 'Airport Security Act,' which would make it illegal for all but law enforcement to carry loaded guns onto airport property. He stated his socialist rationale - *"Only law enforcement officials should be allowed to carry loaded weapons in the unsecured sections of our nation's airports, [because] over time, we have seen evidence that our airports are increasingly vulnerable to small-scaled attacks by armed gunmen."*[300]

It is unmistakable that research suggests some criminals select their targets based on the targets' vulnerable position. It should be noted that I will not probe into the vast body of research on the psychological motives of criminals within the confines of this essay.

The data on the subject of the effectiveness of 'Gun Free Zone' signs is a mixed bag at best and depends entirely on the researcher's definition of what constitutes a mass shooting. The FBI and the United States Congressional Research Service both acknowledge that there is currently no broadly accepted definition of a public mass shooting. Consequently, some researchers use three or more persons killed or injured. This definition is considerably broad and can include murder-suicides of family members in homes or drug trafficking deals gone wrong in non-public locations. Still, other researchers use a very narrow definition, investigating the locations of the shootings and talking to witnesses to create granular criteria from which to make a determination. This narrow definition is used to weed out events and other activities that may skew the research data. Moreover, the FBI has attempted to provide some minimal guidance with an all-purpose definition of a 'public mass shooting,' as one in which four or more people selected indiscriminately, not including the perpetrator, are killed. Nevertheless, it is still based on the researcher to determine.

Using the more stringent criteria, John Lott Jr, a renowned researcher at the Crime Prevention Research Center (CPRC), found that since 1950, 98.4 percent or all but two public mass shootings in America took place where the average citizen is prohibited from carrying a firearm.[301] The Heritage Foundation, using the Stanford Geospatial Center's dataset of mass shootings, defined mass shootings as four or more fatalities in a 24-hour period involving a shooter targeting the public at random who were not relations or adversaries of the attempted murderer. Based on these criteria, the Heritage Foundation found that 54 of the 153 incidents, or 35 percent, met the selected criteria. Of the 54 incidents, the shooter chose locations where guns were banned 37 times, or 69 percent of the time.[302] Leaving 17 times or 31 percent of the shootings occurring where guns were legally permitted. And of the remaining 17 times, or 31 percent, five times, or 29 percent, ended when the gunman was stopped or slowed by a gun permit holder's intervention.[303] Obtaining the Stanford Geospatial Center's dataset of mass shootings, I performed a similar data analysis, resulting in outcomes comparable to those of the Heritage Foundation.

> *"My skepticism about gun laws is criminals don't follow the law. They don't care what the law is, you can pass any law you want and criminals won't follow it."* ~ Senator Marco Rubio.

While some may debate the merits of the "Gun Free Zone" signs or the definition of a mass shooting, the overarching research continues to point to the fact that most random mass shootings happen within areas where firearms are not permitted. If we are intellectually honest, this would explain why mass shootings rarely occur at police stations, gun shows, and gun ranges—further explaining why gun control advocates don't place gun-free zone signs in the front yards of their homes.

It's the Guns Fault...Really?

Jean-Luc, all too often proponents of gun control, use gun ownership as it correlates to homicides as a means to justify their position. They argue that more guns equal more homicides and further claim to have a blizzard of data to substantiate their assertion. In the modern era, focus has been placed on the tool used to cause death rather than the act itself. If guns kill people, then the logical question to follow would be: what made some firearms decide to kill while other firearms decided to remain peaceful? Do firearm manufacturers make homicidal guns? What are the warning signs or triggers to spot a homicidal gun?

It is a fact that gun homicides have declined in recent years; according to DOJ's Bureau of Justice Statistics, U.S. gun-related homicides dropped 49 percent from 1992 through 2011. Major cities of 100,000 or more residents experienced the most significant decline of 23 percent in homicide rates from 2002 to 2011, compared to communities with less than 100,000 inhabitants[304] However, as immense as these numbers are, I will examine the "It's the guns' fault" argument, not in light of gun ownership or gun confiscation, but in light of gun homicide magnitude.

Gun control advocates claim guns are the number one killers in America, or at least the media has drawn significant attention to gun homicides and fashioned that narrative. However, heart disease is the number one cause of death in America, along with cancer as number two. Furthermore, gun homicides are not even in the top 10 causes of death. According to the CDC, the top 10 leading causes of death in the United States are Heart disease at 614,348, Cancer at 591,699, Chronic lower respiratory diseases at 147,101, Accidents (unintentional injuries) at 136,053, Stroke (cerebrovascular diseases) at 133,103, Alzheimer's disease at 93,541, Diabetes at 76,488, Influenza and Pneumonia at 55,227, Nephritis- nephrotic syndrome and nephrosis at 48,146, and Intentional self-harm (suicide) at 42,773. Now, once you add in deaths from unintentional falls at 31,959, motor vehicle traffic deaths at 33,736, unintentional poisoning deaths at 42,032, and all other deaths, the total reached an estimated 2,626,418 in 2014.[305]

If you turn attention to the number of gun homicides as defined by the DOJ's Bureau of Justice Statistics, as murder or the willful killing of one human being by another (including mass shootings), in 2014, the CDC reported there were only 10,945 deaths by homicide. Consequently, gun homicides are only 4 percent of all total deaths in a year. Further, they account for 0.0036 percent of the entire population.

So, I am returning you to the questions asked earlier. If guns kill people, then what made these 10,945 firearms decide to kill while the other estimated 357 million[306] firearms decided to remain peaceful? Do firearm manufacturers make homicidal guns? What are the warning signs or triggers to spot homicidal guns? We can even go further. Why do gun control advocates and liberals concentrate so much energy on confiscating guns and not automobiles, which kill three times more people per year? Moreover, why not place talent and political muscle to fight heart disease, which kills 56 times more people per year than guns?

Furthermore, the gun control proponents' argument that more guns equal more homicides somehow does not match up with the numbers. There are an estimated 357 million[307] guns in the US. That number would have to go up exponentially for the gun homicide rates to double. Even then, heart disease and automobile deaths would still outpace gun homicides. This means gun control proponents appear to be more interested in disarming the citizenry rather than protecting or stopping deaths.

Conclusion

Gun control, in a nutshell, is simply an attempt to socialize the right of self-defense and to place such self-defense in the hands of the government's collective security. Gun control

Gregory E. Parker

advocates use this to merely redistribute gun ownership into the hands of only the police, military, and selected politically connected lawmakers. This makes it very clear that socialists do not seek to protect anyone. Gun control advocates are more interested in disarming the citizenry than stopping deaths. Jean-Luc, what is unmistakably lost on these advocates is that individual freedom for safety afforded by firearms outweighs the collective safety offered by the government. The hypocrisy and lies pushed within identity politics display the gun control advocates ignorance of the very foundation of their argument, in which they seek to socialize a fundamental natural right.

Chapter 5

ISLAM AND THE LIBERAL HYPOCRISY

In 2009, A U.S. Muslim army major, Nidal Malik Hasan, shot and killed 13 people at the Fort Hood Army base. At the climax of the incident, the Obama administration refused to acknowledge the tragic event as a terrorist attack, excusing it instead as workplace violence. Consequently, President Obama took more than six years to identify the major's actions as a terrorist attack publicly, even though Major Hasan continually espoused his Islamic and terroristic intent. Stating he wanted to protect the leader of the Taliban. Retired Army lawyer Jeffrey Addicott, head of the St. Mary's Center for Terrorism Law, noted that *"Apologists for Hasan can no longer assert the false narrative that this was not motivated by radical Islamic extremism."*[308]

In 2015, Elton Simpson and Nadir Soofi began shooting at the Curtis Culwell Center in Garland in hopes of killing anyone tied to the Muhammad cartoon contest. Police officers killed each shooter before any carnage could take place. Islamic State in Iraq and Syria (ISIS) claimed responsibility for the unsuccessful attack. The Obama administration and other Islam apologists' excuses range anywhere from holding the organizers of the event to criticizing the Curtis Culwell Center itself for allowing the event to take place. The administration's goal of its criticism appeared to be to protect others within Islam from any retaliation. Homeland Security Secretary Jeh Johnson stated, *"We urge that members of the public not misdirect anger and suspicion at those simply because of their [Islamic] religious faith."*[309]

In 2014, Alton Nolen beheaded a woman, Colleen Huff, and stabbed two others at an Oklahoma food plant. The media and Islam apologists excused the tragic event as another case of workplace violence, given Nolen was fired days before.[310] To this day, Islam apologists still claim Nolen's motives are unclear, despite the fact that his social media pages appear littered with pro-Islam posts and antisemitic rants.[311]

Jean-Luc, it is apparent from these examples and the ridiculous and ill-conceived justifications for violent unlawful behavior made by Islam apologists, that there is an unmistakable partnership between liberals and Islam. This partnership's true intent is not the advancement of religious equality but the furtherance of the destruction of the U.S. and other Western countries. With that said, I believe it essential to examine the subject of the liberal partnership with Islam and, by extension, liberal hypocrisy. However, before I do, it is prudent to review the background of Islam. Therefore, what follows is my humble understanding of the issue. It is also worth noting that I use the terms 'Islam' and 'Muslim' quite interchangeably within the context of this essay.

Islam

While some concerns exist about the reliability of early sources, nearly all historians agree that Islam originated in Mecca and Medina at the start of the 7th century. Islam began with Muhammad after he claimed to receive a revelation from Allah through the angel Gabriel in the year 610. He soon began to preach that he alone was the prophet of God. Although Muhammad had been an orphan as a child and later became a prosperous businessman, his message of submission to him as the only prophet of God was not well received by the residents of Mecca. Even his uncle rejected his message. Therefore, Muhammad cursed him and his wife, as you can see from his writings *"May the hands of Abu Lahab be ruined, and ruined is he. His wealth will not avail him or that which he gained. He will [enter to] burn in a Fire of [blazing] flame, And his wife [as well] - the carrier of firewood. Around her neck is a rope of [twisted] fiber."* ~ Quran 111:1–5.

In Mecca, Muhammad's teachings began to foster a great division between those who believed in his teachings (believers) and those who did not (nonbelievers), I.E., the Muslims and the infidels.[312] With his aggressive and pushy style, Muhammad found very little success in convincing or

converting Meccans of his divine nature or to see the equality
of his God. He was exiled from Mecca after his uncle died,
relocating to Medina, where things began to change. After
entering Medina, Muhammad changed Islam to include jihad
or struggle against the enemies of Islam. Through this jihad
and the fear that it created, Muhammad gained money and,
by extension, political power. This newfound political power
and success, along with his anger from the rejection at Mecca,
created a very vengeful political leader, to the point
Muhammed personally involved himself in violent raids and
battles on the tribes of his enemies. These victories allowed
Muhammed to further perfect his image as the only prophet
leader for God, enacting God's will and displaying the duality
of his religion.

> *"Muhammed had a very dualistic personality. He had a sense of
> humor, he loved children. He wept when his favorite warrior was
> killed. But at the same time, he was a soft-spoken man who
> laughed heartily when the head of one of his enemies was thrown
> at his feet. He financed jihad through the sale of slaves."*[313]

As a spiritual leader in Mecca for thirteen years,
Muhammad only converted 150 people to his religion. In
contrast, as a successful but vengeful political leader in
Medina, Muhammad's religion of Islam, using jihad, grew
extremely large, and Muhammad became a king in ten
years.[314] Today, Muhammad is considered, within Islam, to be
the perfect Muslim. His life is to be an example that all
Muslims must follow. He is considered the perfect husband,

religious leader, military leader, and political leader. All the details of how to be a good Muslim are found in Muhammad's example as well as in the Quran.

Moreover, Islam has three holy books: the Quran or religious text, the Sira, Muhammad's biography and Hadith, and small stories or traditions from Muhammad. The latter two books make up the Sunna. It is also worth noting that the Quran is not arranged sequentially. When organized in sequential order, it is unmistakable that a transition occurred following Muhammad's move to Medina. Conceptually, this change can be seen as a conversion from Mecca's aggressive peace to Medina's vengeful supremacy.[315]

That brings me to the two faces of Islam. This particular view of Islam is not new and has been put forth in several books and articles. Conversely, I, too, assert that Islam has two faces: Mecca, an aggressive although peaceful face, and Medina, the vengeful political warrior face. Muslims and their apologist actively quote passages that make Islam appear loving and harmless. These peaceful and gentle verses from the Quran were written in Muhammad's early days in Mecca when his methods were aggressive but primarily peaceful.

> *"As to those who reject faith, I will punish them with terrible agony in this world and in the Hereafter, nor will they have anyone to help." ~ Quran 3:56*

> *"I will cast terror into the hearts of those who disbelieve. Therefore strike off their heads and strike off every fingertip of them" ~ Quran 8:12*

"Fight those who believe not in Allah nor the Last Day, nor hold that forbidden which hath been forbidden by Allah and His Messenger, nor acknowledge the religion of Truth, (even if they are) of the People of the Book, until they pay the Jizya with willing submission, and feel themselves subdued." ~ Quran 9:29

"And when We wish to destroy a town, We send Our commandment to the people of it who lead easy lives, but they transgress therein; thus the word proves true against it, so We destroy it with utter destruction." ~ Quran 17:16

However, Muslims and their apologist conveniently bypass the passages listed above that instruct Muslims to kill nonbelievers, commit acts of terrorism, and foster division and religious intolerance, which Muhammad wrote in later years when his methods were considerably more bloody in Medina. The Quran contains some 109 verses that call Muslims to commit violent acts against nonbelievers. Several are somewhat graphic, with instructions to behead, amputate limbs, and kill nonbelievers wherever they hide.

"And kill them wherever you overtake them and expel them from wherever they have expelled you, and fitnah is worse than killing. And do not fight them at al-Masjid al-Haram until they fight you there. But if they fight you, then kill them. Such is the recompense of the disbelievers" ~ Quran 2:191

Muslims who do not join the fight are referred to as hypocrites and warned that Allah will send them to hell. Upon closer reflection of Muhammad's life, we can ascertain a pattern that has emerged in the modern era of Islam. As noted above, while somewhat peaceful, Mohammed, through his daily preaching and argumentative style, created division and anger among the people of Mecca.[316] We can see this division and anger in most Western countries today that have a large Muslim immigrant population. Moreover, the Medina or vengeful political warrior face reflects today's political terrorism.

Islam in the World

Now that I have briefly examined the history of Islam and presented its two faces, you can now assess what that means in today's society. To obtain a clearer understanding of the two faces of Islam, I believe it is first prudent to examine the term moderate Muslim. Merriam-Webster's dictionary defines moderate as avoiding extremes of behavior or observing reasonable limits. Western, highly secularized societies consider religious truths to be flexible or simply non-existent, making moderate spirituality possible and fervent followers of such spirituality extremists. The classic mistake here for Western societies is to assume such moderation equates to liberalism or progressivism.

> "*Fight those who do not believe in Allah or in the Last Day and who do not consider unlawful what Allah and His Messenger have made unlawful and who do not adopt the religion of truth from*

those who were given the Scripture - [fight] until they give the jizyah willingly while they are humbled." ~ Quran 9:29

In the modern era, the term moderate Muslim is rarely challenged, yet it is commonly used post-terrorist attack as a mantra to push the agenda of identity politics and victimhood. Islam apologists are more concerned with racism, xenophobia, or hurting the feelings of Muslims rather than the attack or its actual victims. We can see this as the media parade a litany of Muslim individuals on talk shows to denounce a terror attack and claim their families are in danger of reprisal from racists. Such reprisals rarely come to fruition. British Muslim boxer Amir Khan appeared on the Good Morning Britain TV show to denounce the Manchester suicide bombing that killed 22 people and that he fears fellow Muslims, including his two-year-old daughter, will be targeted by racists because of the terrorist attack. *"I am Muslim, and if I'm on the bus or train, I don't want them pointing at me saying, we don't want to be on the train with you. I think Muslims all have to stick together; in all different religions, there is always good and bad."*[317] A similar Muslim "victim" sentiment was not lost on social media.

> *"The Manchester tag is making me sick, the amount of racism and bullshit people are spouting when they don't know ANYTHING."*[318] *~ POSER (@codyfrostmusic).*

"While you're all refreshing your timelines waiting for updates from Manchester, use your time to report racist and racially abusive tweets"[319] ~ Michelle Sammet (@michellesammet).

In an article for the Guardian, Sarfraz Manzoor spoke to Muslims about the term moderate. He noted that the word moderate means something different to each Muslim, yet the common idea that resonated was that it was an offense to each. One woman he spoke with stated, *"I see it as a criticism. You are giving me this label based on how I look and how I dress."* A Muslim man he spoke with stated he found the term offensive: *"Are you saying I'm only 50% Muslim? When someone says to me 'you're moderate,' it suggests to me they're saying 'you're not fully Muslim.'"*[320]

According to the Pew Research Center, Islam is the second largest religion in the world, with 1.6 billion Muslims, or 23 percent of the global population.[321] That number is expected to equal Christianity by 2050, resulting in 2.8 billion Muslims and 2.9 billion Christians.[322] The Pew Research Center estimates as of 2015, there were 3.3 million Muslims in the U.S., or about 1% of the U.S. population.[323] Data shows 88 percent of Muslims in Egypt, 62% in Pakistan, 86% in Jordan, and 51% in Nigeria believe that any Muslim who chooses to leave Islam should be put to death. Comparable, if not identical, numbers are in favor of stoning people who commit adultery, severely punishing those who criticize Muhammad or Islam, and chopping off hands for theft. These practices are a part of the penal code of Islamic law, known as Sharia

Law.[324] Furthermore, 84% of Muslims in South Asia, 77% in Southeast Asia, 74% in the Middle East and North Africa, and 64% in Sub-Saharan Africa support Sharia as the law of the land.[325] According to a poll done by the Center for Security Policy, 51% of American Muslims agree that they should be able to forego the Constitution and be governed instead by Sharia law.

As a result of this data, anecdotal and quantitative, it is clear there are no "moderate" Muslims, as most, if not all, Muslims believe in the Quran and Sharia law. Given that moderate is a falsehood in Islam, the question then becomes whether or not the individual Muslim is willing to kill for their beliefs (Medina) or whether the individual Muslim will seek non-violent conquest (Mecca). The term radical or extremist Islam is a term derived from those who are ignorant of Islam. Abubaker Shariff Ahmed, a Kenyan cleric, stated after the Nairobi Westgate shopping mall terror attack where 67 people were killed, some women and children, that *"Radical Islam is a creation of people who do not believe in Islam. We don't have radical Islam, we don't have moderates, we don't have extremists. Islam is one religion following the Koran and the Sunna."*[326]

Within these two faces of Islam, non-violent Muslims (Mecca) will maintain a justified horror at the acts of terrorism committed by violent Muslims (Medina) while benefiting from the terrorist act itself. I.E., both non-violent and violent Muslims share two essential goals: to convert non-believers to Islam and to silence critics of Islam. The two faces of Islam assist in achieving these aims by operating in an atmosphere of ignorance, compliance, and political correct Marxism.

There are two primary tactics Muslims actively use to convert non-believers and or silence critics, thereby perpetuating the spread of Islam and creating an atmosphere of ignorance and compliance. The Mecca face was one of peaceful aggression that manifested in the form of pursuing legislation, litigation, identity politics, and or politically correct Marxism. It should be noted that a combination of all these tactics can and are commonly used to convert non-believers and or silence critics. At the same time, the Medina face has manifested itself in the form of actual political terrorism.

Let's first examine the violent tactics being employed to actively instill fear to convert non-believers to Islam and silence its critics, which is most commonly done through the use of political terrorism.

> "Indeed, the penalty for those who wage war against Allah and His Messenger and strive upon earth [to cause] corruption is none but that they be killed or crucified or that their hands and feet be cut off from opposite sides or that they be exiled from the land. That is for them a disgrace in this world; and for them in the Hereafter is a great punishment" ~ Quran 9:29

Two masked gunmen brandishing AK 47s and rocket launchers attacked the headquarters of the French satirical newspaper Charlie Hebdo and killed 12 people. The killings were in retaliation for the newspaper's depiction of the prophet Muhammad. The newspaper was previously firebombed for similar cartoons. Defiant and a supporter of the freedom of speech, the paper's editor, Stephane Charbonnie, stated before his death, *"I am not afraid of retaliation. I have no children, no wife, no car, no credit. It perhaps sounds a bit pompous, but I'd rather die standing than live on my knees."*[327] This freedom of speech was once a centerpiece of the liberal movement. The idea is that an individual is free to speak truth to power. However, such speech is now branded as "hate speech" or viewed by liberals as a physical assault upon their person. As noted in my essay *"Freedom and Democratic Socialism,"* it is very natural to want to protect oneself from harm, and society has an innate desire to seek safety or being safe from harm, and that desire for safety (collective safety) will always lead to reduced individual freedom. Therefore, there is an apparent socialist intent to silence criticism of this liberal perceived harm or perceived physical assault. This socialist intent to silence criticism reinforces the Islamic religion as it seeks to spread its dominance. Thereby creating a "blame the victim" mindset for not curtailing their speech or blaming the woman for her rape because she was not modest in her choice of wardrobe. We see this mentality in the responses to the Charlie Hebdo massacre.

Consequently, liberals blamed the editor for the slaughter. Bill Donohue, the president of the Catholic League for Religious and Civil Rights, in a statement entitled *"Muslims are right to be angry,"* stated that Charlie Hebdo had *"intolerance and its journalists' disgusting record of playing a role in causing their own death."*[328] I.E., if they had not drawn the cartoons of Muhammad, they would not have died.

Further, it is this liberal perceived harm or perceived physical assault from the lack of freedom of religion for Muslims that causes Islam apologists to justify the terror attacks as warranted. Much the same way liberals justify riots and looting in the black community.[329]

While the worldwide terror attacks are too many to list within the pages of this book, they are all unambiguous examples of the Medina face of Islam. The goal of these attacks is to make nonbelievers fear and capitulate to the Islamic religion. Foreign leaders have done just that. Emmanuel Macron, the French President, stated that terrorism is an *"imponderable problem which will be part of our daily lives for the years to come."*[330] His comments echo former Prime Minister Manuel Valls's statement following the Nice lorry attack in 2016, which killed 87. *"Times have changed, and we should learn to live with terrorism."*[331] Chancellor Angela Merkel said that Germans have fundamentally failed to understand how Muslim immigration has altered their country and will have to come to grips with more mosques than churches throughout the countryside. *"Our country is going to carry on changing, and integration is also a task for the society taking up the task of dealing with immigrants. For years we've been deceiving ourselves about this. Mosques, for example, are going to be a more prominent part of our cities than they were before."*[332]

Second, aggressive yet non-violent tactics being employed to convert non-believers to Islam and silence critics is through methods such as legislation, litigation, or identity politics, I.E., politically correct Marxism. Pure political terrorism is designed to result in fear, apprehension, and capitulation quickly, while legislation, litigation, and identity politics are designed to create division and surrender over time. Especially in Western democracies where hiding behind the push for religious equality will, over time, erode individual freedom and foster ignorance and surrender. Muslims will continue to demand more and more equality, thereby dividing the nation against itself. Pamela Geller, founder and publisher of The Geller Report, stated in an article that Muslims are never satisfied, and their demands invariably lead to more submission. *"Accommodation to Muslim demands gives way to more demands, more submission."*[333]

While the Quran communicates that violent actions against those who speak out against Islam are acceptable, I argue that violent actions are not always needed to decapitate or dominate nonbelievers. Islam uses legislation, litigation, or identity politics, I.E., politically correct Marxism, to create significant distortions on the individual freedom of nonbelievers. See my essay on *"Freedom and Democrat Socialism"* for an understanding of distortions on individual freedom. Under the declaration of the public good or collective security, liberals will push the government to wrongly pursue a strategy of equalizing religious freedom for Muslims at the expense of all other religious groups.[334] These government distortions on freedom targeting the nonbelievers are evident in today's society and currently appear to be a coordinated effort. The Center for Security Policy (CSP) warned in 2015 that the United States Council of Muslim Organizations (USCMO), deceptively cloaked in red, white, and blue, is simply the leading edge of the Islamic Movement in the United States. Their operations include tactics learned directly from the KGB, enabling its organization to accumulate gradually into American society. These include academia, the U.S. judicial system, faith groups, all levels of government, the media, intelligence and security agencies, refugee resettlement and immigration. Further, the group's Secretary-General is directly connected to Saul Alinsky's Industrial Areas Foundation (IAF), a Marxist organization dedicated to the destruction of America.[335]

In an obvious example, a female Muslim student, with the support of the Council on American-Islamic Relations (CAIR), is now suing the Citadel, a military college that has operated for 175 years and has not allowed an exception to its dress code, to allow her to wear a hijab with the military uniform. Citadel spokeswoman Kim Keelor stated, *"Is it the first such request that has been made,....."*[336] Another private military academy has offered to allow female Muslim students to wear their hijab as they wish. However, the cadet explained that is not acceptable to her. This comparable offer is not acceptable to the cadet, given her goal is not actually to participate at the school; her aim undoubtedly is to further the Islamic agenda and change the school's culture through the court system.

In another example, a Muslim woman was pulled over by Dearborn Heights, Michigan, police and arrested for having a suspended license and two outstanding warrants for her arrest. While in custody, she was forced to remove her hijab. She is now suing the police department, with the support of the Council on American-Islamic Relations, for religious discrimination. Her attorney Amir Makled, stated, *"The main issue here is that my client's constitutional rights, her religious liberties, can't be stripped at the jailhouse door. She has an absolute right to maintain her faith. We hope this cause of action will bring to light a policy that is dated and needs to be amended… We also hope to get some further diversity training for officers in the city. Hopefully, this will be a learning experience for other law enforcement agencies."*[337] Despite the fact that other prisoners or detainees are forced to remove their hats, caps, and other items for identification and officer safety. Her fight is undoubtedly not about religious equality; she already has that. Her goal is to subjugate the Dearborn Heights police department into changing its policy and thereby furthering the Islamic agenda. Moreover, countless other religious discrimination suits have been filed nationwide.

Legislation, litigation, or identity politics as a bullying tactic can also be seen in other countries. The Canadian Liberal politicians passed a motion to condemn Islamophobia. Conservative Canadian politician Brad Trost stated the motion and subsequent instruction to the Canadian government to study ways to address racism and discrimination towards Muslims *"will only serve to strengthen extremist elements within the Muslim community itself that seek to preserve and promote their own form of hate and intolerance.* "[338] Part of the motions reads:

> *"The government should: (a) recognize the need to quell the increasing public climate of hate and fear; (b) condemn Islamophobia and all forms of systemic racism and religious discrimination and take note of House of Commons' petition e-411 and the issues raised by it; and (c) request that the Standing Committee on Canadian Heritage undertake a study on how the government could (i) develop a whole-of-government approach to reducing or eliminating systemic racism and religious discrimination including Islamophobia, in Canada ..."* [339]

Lorne Gunter, an Edmonton Sun columnist, summed up the opposition to the motion as truly one-sided and poised to be a key to stifling free speech and objective criticism, *"While purporting to oppose all forms of religious discrimination, the only form specifically mentioned is Islamophobia. And no definition of Islamophobia is given, leaving the door wide open to the broadest possible interpretations – including public statements condemning radical Islamic terrorism and even academic papers questioning whether Islam truly is a religion of peace."* [340]

If you take a look back, not so far in the distant past, you can see that atheists and liberals have fought tooth and nail to remove any religious symbols or context from public schools. These atheist activists and liberal judges set out to wipe religion from public schools. The case of Freedom From Religion Foundation v. Concord Community Schools, where a federal judge ordered an Indiana high school to halt a live Nativity musical that had been enjoyed since 1970, calling it an unconstitutional example of religious indoctrination imposing its cruelty on children vulnerable to religious conversion. Judge Jon E. Deguilio, a liberal appointee, concluded that *"a reasonable observer would fairly believe that the portrayal of the living nativity scene, when viewed in the particular context, circumstances, and history of the Christmas Spectacular, conveys a message of endorsement of religion, or that a particular religious belief is favored or preferred."*[341]

The San Diego Unified School District administrators, in an effort to battle Islamophobia, have instituted a plan to provide teachers and students with calendars showing Islamic holidays. Students will be required to learn more about Islam in social studies classes, and Muslims will be provided safe places on campus. Stan Anjan, executive director of the district's Family and Community Engagement, stated, *"It's more of a comprehensive program, not just a curriculum. We're looking at it from a very integrated and holistic approach."*[342] These distortions on freedom by the government are distinct and designed to benefit only one group of people. There is no activity by School District administrators to offer safe places for Christians or Mormons. Further, no extra effort by School District officials is being made to require students to learn more about Buddhism in social studies classes.

In another example, two mothers expressed discontent with the Chatham Board of Education concerning the school district not adhering to its policy prohibiting 'proselytizing' in the classroom. The parents pointed out that the instruction in the seventh-grade class included a video elucidation of the Five Pillars of Islam. The video also featured lines like "Allah is the creator of everything, the one true God."[343] Liberal and atheists have fought for years and were successful in removing other religions from public schools, yet are notably silent on Islam in public schools. Further, while liberals and atheist activists were endeavoring to cleanse every inch of Christianity out of public schools, Islamic religious practices have been thrust as part of public school curricula nationwide since 2003. As evidenced by the Eklund v. Byron Union School District case, parents in Northern California sued over a middle school world history program. The program featured a series of activities in which students were required to "become a Muslim" for three weeks, told to choose a Muslim name, recite Islamic prayers, and participate in imaginary pilgrimages to Mecca. An unpublished opinion in the 9th Circuit concluded that the school's teaching about Islam did not encompass "overt religious exercises" that would violate church-state separation.[344]

In another example, a 42-year-old man from Jutland, Denmark, is being charged with blasphemy for burning the Quran in his backyard. His attorney speculates this prosecution is driven by the government's fear of Muslim extremists. His lawyer further noted that it is entirely legal to burn a Bible in Denmark, highlighting the 1997 incident of the Danish artist who set fire to a copy of the Bible on state television in Denmark yet was not charged.[345]

Identity politics works hand and glove with the legislation and or litigation tactic, albeit the motive is to induce 'moral paralysis' and actualize public outcry around declaring victim status for Muslims. The perceived harm due to the lack of religious freedom for Muslims causes Islam apologists to justify the need for more significant legislative or judicial restrictions on the individual liberties of non-believers and guilt them into inaction and silence. This moral paralysis is without a doubt seen as Muslims argue Islamophobia for anyone who dares speak out against Islam. Such identity politics are enormously destructive because it is entirely artificial and built on the premise that individual freedom is subordinate to that of the group's religious desires.

Moreover, Muslims continue to cultivate this Western identity politics, inducing 'moral paralysis' by outwardly lying and deceiving nonbelievers. The Quran instructs Muslims to lie in the furtherance of the Islamic faith, even to the point of gaining the trust of non-believers in order to ascertain vulnerability and defeat or kill the enemy. Several forms of lying are permitted to non-believers—the most well-known being "Taqiyya," which is any circumstance that advances the cause of Islam. The Taqiyya will allow Muslims to lie, plot against, and deceive non-believers (coworkers, leaders, friends) as long as they do not take the lie to heart, and it is in the furtherance of Islam. The word "makara," used in the Quran passages below, is the Arabic word for scheme or plot, which literally means "deceit." Therefore, if Allah is supremely deceitful toward any and all unbelievers, it would stand to reason that Muslims are allowed to do the same.

"Allah will not call you to account for that which is unintentional in your oaths, but He will call you to account for that which your hearts have earned. And Allah is Oft-Forgiving, Most-Forbearing."~ Quran (2:225).

"And they (disbelievers) plotted [to kill 'Iesa (Jesus)], and Allah planned too. And Allah is the Best of the planners." ~ Quran (3:54).

"And (remember) when the disbelievers plotted against you (O Muhammad) to imprison you, or to kill you, or to get you out (from your home, i.e. Makkah); they were plotting and Allah too was planning, and Allah is the Best of the planners." ~ Quran (8:30).

"And when We let mankind taste of mercy after some adversity has afflicted them, behold! They take to plotting against Our Ayat (proofs, evidences, verses, lessons, signs, revelations, etc.)! Say: "Allah is more Swift in planning!" Certainly, Our Messengers (angels) record all of that which you plot." ~ Quran (10:21).

"That she heard Allah's Apostle saying, "He who makes peace between the people by inventing good information or saying good things, is not a liar." ~ Sahih Bukhari (49:857)

This deceit has never been more evident than in the San Bernardino massacre, where 17 people were killed and 14 more were injured. What makes this an obvious example of such deceit is that the terrorists were well thought of co-workers of those killed. The gunmen worked with, associated with, and were even given a baby shower by coworkers. However, the couple, Syed Farook, 28, and his new wife, Tashfeen Malik, 27, both devout Muslims, stormed out of an office Christmas party only to return to inflict carnage. Griselda Reisinger, a former co-worker, stated, *"He [Farook] was very quiet. I would say hi and bye, but we never engaged him in conversation. He didn't say much at all. [He]..never struck me as a fanatic, he never struck me as suspicious."*[346] In another example of deceit, Yasmin Seweid, a female Muslim student at Baruch College, claimed that three men assaulted her on a New York Manhattan subway by ripping off her hijab. She told the police that three white men screaming "Donald Trump!" attacked her on an uptown train.[347] Seweid's story, after investigation, was later found to be a hoax, and she was arrested and charged with filing a false report. Female Muslim students at San Diego State University and the University of Louisiana at Lafayette perpetrated similar hoaxes. Both reported two men shouting pro-Trump rhetoric after ripping off their hijabs. All garnered national attention and protest after the Council on American-Islamic Relations (CAIR) became involved. In the University of Louisiana incident, Lafayette Police stated: *"[the complainant]...admitted that she fabricated the story about her physical attack as well as the removal of her hijab and wallet by two white males."*[348]

Consequently, as with all singular myopic advocacy, in the beginning, the movement does not clash with other advocacy groups that seek to be the dominant angry victims. Nevertheless, the long-term struggle of the advocacy group to be the dominant victim will forge conflict and cannibalism between other advocacy groups. This conflict is already starting to display itself. The Maryland-based Service Employees International Union (SEIU) Local 500 filed a charge of unfair labor practices against the Council on American-Islamic Relations (CAIR). SEIU claims the Islamic civil rights group blocked union organizers' admission to the workplace, made threatening and coercive statements to employees ahead of an organizing vote, and fired at least three employees for attempting to organize workers. SEIU Local 500 spokesman Christopher Honey stated, *"...there is so much union busting going on over there that it is impossible to have a fair election. The whole things seems totally antithetical to what they do with their work at CAIR."*[349]

Islam and Women's Rights

In this modern era, son, the debate over Islam and its oppression of women is not whether such oppression exists. It is merely a debate as to what level of oppression is permitted. According to the Merriam-Webster dictionary, feminism is defined as a theory of the political and economic belief that men and women should have equal rights and opportunities structured around activities supporting women's rights. In this essay, we will focus our analysis and comparison to the "third wave" of feminism that started in the mid to late 1980s with its focus on issues of patriarchy and its contention that men inherently seek to subjugate and exploit women systematically.

Modern-era feminists recognize misogyny, a dislike of, contempt for, or ingrained prejudice against women, and sexism, a prejudice, stereotyping, or discrimination, typically against women, in every aspect of everyday life. From feminists calling the equation "E=mc2" sexist because of the privileges of the speed of light[350] to the cries of misogyny for "slut-shaming," the act of criticizing sexually promiscuous women.[351] Further, feminists argue it is misogynistic or sexist to criticize a woman for not wanting to have sex.[352] While several of these examples seem contradictory and extreme, it does go to the broader point, whether intentional or involuntary, to see the prejudice found by feminists.

Therefore, with this heightened level of sensitivity to misogyny and sexism by feminists, it is hard to comprehend the coupling of feminism and Islam. In Islam, such misogyny, sexism, and the devaluing of women are mathematically established.

> *"Allah commands you as regards your children's (inheritance); to the male, a portion equal to that of two females; if (there are) only daughters, two or more, their share is two-thirds of the inheritance; if only one, her share is half. For parents, a sixth share of inheritance to each if the deceased left children; if no children, and the parents are the (only) heirs, the mother has a third; if the deceased left brothers or (sisters), the mother has a sixth. (The*

distribution in all cases is) after the payment of legacies he may have bequeathed or debts. You know not which of them, whether your parents or your children, are nearest to you in benefit, (these fixed shares) are ordained by Allah. And Allah is Ever All-Knower, All-Wise." ~ Quran 4:11.

"Allah directs (thus) about Al-Kalalah (those who leave neither descendants nor ascendants as heirs). If it is a man that dies, leaving a sister, but no child, she shall have half the inheritance. If (such a deceased was) a woman, who left no child, her brother takes her inheritance. If there are two sisters, they shall have two-thirds of the inheritance; if there are brothers and sisters, the male will have twice the share of the female. (Thus) does Allah makes clear to you (His Law) lest you go astray? And Allah is the All-Knower of everything." ~ Quran 4:176.

"And call to witness, from among your men, two witnesses. And if two men be not found then a man and two women." Muslim *apologists offer creative explanations to explain why Allah felt that a man's testimony in court should be valued twice as highly as a woman's, but studies consistently show that women are actually less likely to tell lies than men, meaning that they make more reliable witnesses."* ~ Quran 2:282.

This oppression of women is quite ingrained in the Islamic culture. In Saudi Arabia, women cannot vote, drive, show their faces, or talk with male non-relatives in public. Women are required to wear the "Hijab," an Islamic head covering, and adhere to other religious dress codes of modesty.

"And tell the believing women to reduce [some] of their vision and guard their private parts and not expose their adornment except

*that which [necessarily] appears thereof and to wrap [a portion of]
their head covers over their chests and not expose their adornment
except to their husbands, their fathers, their husbands 'fathers,
their sons, their husbands' sons, their brothers, their brothers
'sons, their sisters' sons, their women, that which their right
hands possess, or those male attendants having no physical desire,
or children who are not yet aware of the private aspects of
women. And let them not stamp their feet to make known what
they conceal of their adornment. And turn to Allah in repentance,
all of you, O believers, that you might succeed." ~ Quran 24:31.*

An example of the oppression that Islamic dress
regulations inflict on women came in March of 2002 when
fifteen girls were killed in a fire at their school. Saudi's
religious police, the "Muttawa," battled with police officers
and firemen to keep the girls inside the burning building,
given the girls had shed their all-concealing outer garments,
which would be a transgression of Islamic law.[353]

Regarding rape and sexuality that, feminists prize so
heavily. Rape of Muslim women is against Islamic law. Such a
restriction on rape does not mean it does not occur. Moreover,
the all too common rape of a Muslim woman is almost
impossible to prove under strict Islamic law, given the
testimony of a woman is worth less than a man's. Women
would need to provide four male witnesses to substantiate
her claim.

*"And those who accuse chaste women and then do not produce
four witnesses - lash them with eighty lashes and do not accept*

from them testimony ever after. And those are the defiantly disobedient." ~ Quran 24:4.

Islamic law disregards forensic evidence, favoring the use of eyewitness testimony instead. If the woman accuser does not provide four male witnesses to her rape, a man can simply claim the act was consensual or that the sexual act did not take place, thereby leaving the woman branded as an adulterer. With adulterer's death or honor killings may be used. As evidenced by an Iranian man cutting off his seven-year-old daughter's head after suspecting her uncle had raped her, thereby *"defending my honor, family, and dignity."*[354] However, the post-death investigation showed the girl to be a virgin still.[355] According to the Human Rights Commission of Pakistan, between January 2004 and January 2017, there were 8955 honor killings of women, I.E., two women are killed every day by male relatives seeking to avenge the family's honor. This "blame the victim" mentality places all the burden of avoiding sexual encounters on the woman, even rape.

However, rape of a non-Muslim woman is permitted and encouraged. Suad Saleh, an Islamic professor at Al-Azhar University in Cairo, stated in an interview on Al-Hayat TV that Allah makes it permissible for Muslim men to rape non-Muslim women in order to humiliate them. *"The female prisoners of wars are 'those whom you own.' In order to humiliate them, they become the property of the army commander or of a Muslim, and he can have sex with them just like he has sex with his wives,"*[356]

An Imam in Cologne, Germany, in the wake of the sex abuse rampage by Muslims on New Year's Eve in 2015, stated, *"the events ...[which included rape]...were the girls' own fault because they were half-naked and wearing perfume."*[357]

Feminists claim there is a significant rape culture on university campuses and in the Western world as a whole. These same feminists are either silent, complicit, or apologetic about the apparent rape culture of Islam. Some go so far as to join with Islam and blame white males, claiming Islamophobia is just a way for white men to derail the debate. Laurie Penny, a liberal columnist for the Guardian, stated in an article entitled *"This isn't 'feminism It's Islamophobia"* that *"I am infuriated by white men stirring up anti-Muslim prejudice to derail debate on western sexism."*[358] In essence, she is claiming that Western patriarchal white males are fabricating blame onto Muslims to cover for their indiscretions. At the same time, other women accept their fate for the good of the collective social norm. While rape across Europe is increasing at an alarming rate, a girl from Brno, Czech Republic, believed that sexual assault for the sake of her political beliefs is just a price she may have to pay. *"Even if something [rape] happened to me, the physical wounds always end up healing."*[359]

Let's turn our attention to domestic abuse. The Muslim country of Dubai Court of Cassation, in 2002, ruled that a husband has the right to beat his wife in order to discipline her, provided the beating does not damage her bones or deform her body.[360] Islam apologists and feminists argue this fact away by stating the Quran does not mean exactly what it says or that the oppressive nature of Islam is just cultural and limited to a few hard-line followers. Theresa Corbin, a feminist who converted to Islam, stated, *"Surprisingly, Islam turned out to be the religion that appealed to my feminist ideals."*[361]

The feminist construction of domestic violence as a social problem varies and ranges from early constructions focusing on family preservation to later emphasizing mental illness, sex differences, male domination, family conflict, and survival.[362] Examining the feminist agenda as it relates to domestic violence, we can see that feminists emphasize gender and power inequality in opposite-sex relationships. Feminists spotlight the perceived societal communication that sanctions a male's strength, the use of violence and aggression, and the gender roles that dictate how men and women should behave in relationships. Feminists see the root cause of domestic violence as the outcome of society's acceptance of aggressive behavior perpetrated by men. Bell Hooks, feminist and author, stated in her book *"Feminism is for Everybody,"* *"Patriarchal violence in the home is based on the belief that it is acceptable for a more powerful individual to control others through various forms of coercive force."*[363]

As we can plainly see, the feminist ideology is noticeably at odds with Islam, given that Islam deems men to be superior to all women. This male superiority is the Islamic justification for the permitted beating of disobedient women.

*"Men are the maintainers of women because Allah has made some of them to excel others and because they spend out of their property; the good women are therefore obedient, guarding the unseen as Allah has guarded; and (as to) those on whose part you fear desertion, admonish them, and leave them alone in the sleeping-places and **beat** them; then if they obey you, do not seek a way against them; surely Allah is High, Great." ~ Quran 4:34*

*"And take in your hand a green branch and **beat** her with it, and do not break your oath..." ~ Quran 38:44*

As very well defined from the Quran verses listed, Muslim men are instructed to *"beat"* disobedient women. However, some Muslims and their apologists claim these passages in the Quran are misunderstood or abused. They maintain the word beat actually means to "tap lightly" and is not intended to instruct Muslim men in the use of any harm. They further claim some Muslim men use this as an excuse to batter their wives when, in essence, the verse means to tap lightly, and only when a woman is involved in bad or appalling behavior that will tarnish the image of the family or cause harm.[364] As if tap excuses domestic violence lightly.

Notwithstanding, the next series of questions then becomes, who determines what a light tap is, and what is the bad behavior that will tarnish the image of the family or cause harm? The Pakistan Institute of Medical Sciences has found that over 90 percent of Pakistani wives have been struck, beaten, or abused sexually for offenses as simple as cooking an unsatisfactory meal or for failing to give birth to a male child.[365] In Egypt, 29 percent of married adolescents have been beaten by their husbands; of those, 41 percent were beaten during pregnancy. A study in Jordan indicated that 26 percent of reported cases of domestic violence were committed against wives under 18.[366] It is evident from this statistical inference that the threshold for bad behavior that will tarnish the image of the family or cause harm is relatively tiny and very subjective.

Feminists turn a blind eye to the hypocrisy and choose to remain silent about the all-too-frequent abuse. Charlotte Bunch, senior scholar at the Center for Women's Global Leadership at Rutgers University, and other feminists have yet to speak out on the domestic violence within Islam. Moreover, Charlotte Bunch and other feminists were quick to claim that religion and faith can be reconciled with feminism, stating, *"The Methodist Church and the Methodist student movement really put me on the path to feminism. [The church] trained me to lead and to stand up for my principles..."*[367]

Unfortunately, child brides within Islam are a common occurrence. In 2002, researchers in refugee camps in Afghanistan and Pakistan found that half the girls were married by age 13.[368] Ayatollah Khomeini, the Former Supreme Leader of Iran, told the Muslim faithful that marrying a girl before she began menstruating was *"a divine blessing."* He counseled fathers: *"Do your best to ensure that your daughters do not see their first blood in your house."*[369] In an Afghan refugee camp, more than 2 out of 3 second-grade girls were married or engaged.[370] That means virtually all the girls in the camp who were beyond second grade were already

married. Fifty-seven percent of Afghan girls under the age of
16, and many as young as nine, are in arranged marriages.[371]
Iranian girls are permitted to marry as young as nine with
parental consent or at the age of thirteen without consent.[372]
Such marriages are unfortunately not uncommon in the US.
In the State of Virginia, it is still legal for girls as young as 12
to be dragged, pregnant, into a courthouse to wed. This
practice has come under increased scrutiny, thanks to the
Virginia Senator Jill Vogel R-Fauquier.[373]

The minimum age for marriage in most US states is 18.
Parental consent exceptions are made for those younger than
18. In 27 states, there is no set minimum age below 18 with
parental consent. The group Unchained At Last estimates that
nearly a quarter-million children, as young as 12, were
married in the US between 2000 and 2010.[374] This loophole in
American law, along with an ever-increasing Muslim
population, places America on a collision course for an
increase in child marriages and a normalization of pedophilia.
I further contend this normalization of pedophilia, which is
sought by advocates of identity politics and Islam apologists,
is also an effort to soften the palatability of Islam and the
Muslim pedophilia culture and its forced integration
throughout the Western world.

It is estimated that more than 200 million girls and women
alive today have undergone female genital mutilation in the
countries where the practice is concentrated. Furthermore,
there are an estimated 3 million girls at risk of undergoing
female genital mutilation every year. The majority undergo

the procedure before they turn 15 years of age. Female genital mutilation has been documented in 30 countries, mainly in Africa, as well as in the Middle East and Asia.[375] The horror of female genital mutilation takes place in the US as well. Dr. Jumana Nagarwala, Dr. Fakhruddin, and his wife were arrested for performing female genital mutilation on girls as young as six years old at a medical clinic in Livonia, Michigan.[376] Most authorities agree that female circumcision is designed to reduce a woman's sexual desire, making adultery less likely. This logic left a question in my mind. In Islam, if women are mandated to have sexual relations with their husbands whenever they request, according to the Quran, would it not serve a better purpose for a woman to have the desire to do so?

Overall, the violence in Europe that has overtaken women due to Islam is overwhelming. In Europe, especially Sweden, not only has there been a stark increase in violent crimes since it has become the hub of Muslim migration, it is now the rape capital of Europe. However, if we examine deeper, we realize that the sound of feminists' silence concerning the savage Muslim oppression of women has its perverse logic. The silence of feminists to Islam and its blatant abuse towards women is rooted in a self-righteous multicultural relativism. Their silence costs the feminist movement their moral claims of equal dignity and individual freedom for women. Their self-righteous multicultural relativism supersedes any desire to push their cause. In other words, there are no protests or causing an uproar because it would bring light to the fact that feminists are not as bad off in the US as they claim. This undoubtedly would erode their moral superiority over men in the United States.

Furthermore, feminist are not only turning a blind eye and remaining silent on the blatant atrocities taking place, but they are also now actively assisting Muslims in their pursuit to gain power in the US. Karen Hinks, a liberal activist, and Rima Nashashibi, the former vice chair of the Democratic Party of Orange County, formed WELead OC, a group dedicated to building a pipeline of Muslim candidates for office, with the goal of fielding candidates in either the 2018 or 2020 election cycle.[377]

Moreover, as I have stated in my essay 'Identity Politics Feeling Over Facts, ' all singular myopic advocacy seeking to be the dominant angry victim will nevertheless create conflict and cannibalism between other advocacy groups. This partnership, while happy in the beginning, will undoubtedly lead to ruin. The question becomes which group will be victorious.

Undeniably, feminists do not understand that based on Islamic teachings, they, too, will incur subjugation once Muslims obtain power. Feminists are forming alliances with Islam to obtain a passionate voting bloc, which they believe will keep the liberals in power. Nevertheless, the group appears to be intentionally moving women from the ballot box to the burkas.

Islam and Gays

Islam goes beyond merely disapproving of homosexuality. Islamic law instructs that homosexuality is punishable by death. Homosexuals are thrown off buildings, burned, beheaded, hanged, or stoned in Saudi Arabia and Iran, where Islamic laws are applied most strictly. The death penalty for homosexual behavior is on the books in 5 other Muslim countries.

> *"And (remember) Lout (Lot), when he said to his people: Do you commit the worst sin such as none preceding you has committed in the 'Alamin (mankind and jinns)? Verily, you practice your lusts on men instead of women. Nay, but you are a people transgressing beyond bounds (by committing great sins). And the answer of his people was only that they said: Drive them out of your town, these are indeed men who want to be pure (from sins)! Then We saved him and his family, except his wife; she was of those who remained behind (in the torment). And We rained down on them a rain (of stones). Then see what was the end of the Mujrimun (criminals, polytheists, sinners, etc.)." ~ Quran (7:80-84)*

> *"Whoever you find doing the action of the people of Loot, execute the one who does it and the one to whom it is done." ~ Abu Dawud (4462)*

> *[Muhammad said] "Whoever is found conducting himself in the manner of the people of Lot, kill the doer and the receiver." ~ Sunan 1:152*

40 Muslim-majority countries have laws criminalizing homosexuality, offering punishments ranging from fines and short jail sentences to whippings.[378] However, homosexual relationships are not strictly illegal in 20 Muslim-majority nations.[379] Such relationships are significantly frowned upon, and clerics often preach against them. Wael Shihab, an Imam, stated that Muslims should avoid gays, as homosexuality is evil and succumbing to the temptations of Satan. In 2016, A Tunisia Imam explained that he believed harsh penalties should befall gay men and women, *"God is very straightforward about this — not we Muslims, not subjective, the Sharia is very clear about it, the punishment for homosexuality, bestiality or anything like that is death. We don't make any excuses about that; it's not our law — it's the Quran."*[380]

While several countries have the death penalty, and some have even resorted to hurling gay men off of buildings, the US has also been the site of Islam enacting its so-called justice on homosexuals. Omar Mateen, a 29-year-old devout Muslim, killed 50 people and injured 50 more at a popular gay nightclub in Orlando, Florida. Mateen's father stated that religion did not motivate his son, *"This had nothing to do with religion. He saw two men kissing each other in front of his wife and kid, and he got very angry."*[381] Liberals echoed the father's statement in hopes of downplaying the terrorist act and claiming that religion had nothing to do with Mateen's actions. Sally Kohn, an MSNBC personality, stated, *"Every religion has sub-groups of intolerant extremism. You can't tell me the problem is religion. The problem is intolerant extremism!"*[382] Based on this essay, you can unmistakably see the absurdity in these statements.

Conversely, it is clear that liberals have a victim hierarchy within identity politics, and they have chosen to elevate Muslims over gays, feminists, and blacks. Liberals in other countries have decided to elevate Islam over gay rights as well. This elevation is another blatant example of myopic advocacy directly conflicting with other advocacy groups. The Dutch anti-discrimination hotline explained that it is OK for Muslims to threaten gay people. According to Dutch media advisors from the anti-discrimination bureau explained that while homophobic abuse was usually a crime, it was justifiable if you were Muslim due to laws on freedom of religious expression. *"The remarks must be seen in the context of religious beliefs in Islam, which juridically takes away the insulting character."*[383] Moreover, the country of Chechnya opened the world's first concentration camp for homosexuals since Hitler's reign in the 1930s. Human rights activists stress that gay men are being tortured with electric shocks and beaten to death.[384]

Conclusion

Islam's push throughout the world has resulted in the mass slaughter of millions over its 1,400 years of existence.

Nevertheless, Islam apologists endeavor to reassure the American public and the world that tolerance of the violent Muslim religion can make any moderate Muslim assimilate into Westernized culture. Regrettably, even insignificant aspects of Islam are so oppressive that you cannot moderately adhere to Islamic doctrine and somehow coexist with Western civilization. This construct makes the word moderate, as we understand it, nonexistent. Further, if moderation of the Islam religion means you tolerate a relinquishment of individual freedom, then tolerance is nothing more than submission and servitude. This is why the hypocrisy of liberals to push Islam and to advocate for such will only result in enslavement for all.

PARTING THOUGHTS

JEAN-LUC, WHEN I SAT down to pen this collection of essays for posterity, I endeavored to write the truth, not for my ends but to encourage thought and intellectual diversity. Given that to a liberal, diversity of appearance is paramount; however, diversity of thought is akin to heresy; this book needed to be completed for your sake.

Liberals, progressives, socialists, and those who worship at the altar of identity politics will proclaim this book to be short-sighted, misguided, homophobic, islamophobic, transphobic, racist, and a whole host of other names that are all too familiar socialist slogans. Some will also employ the now fashionable criticism that the truthful words within this book amount to some form of physical violence or assault against their person. However, these individuals will not argue my words were untruthful. They will only justify the manner in which these written words made them feel. Thus bringing validity to the very words within these pages.

As you move through life, son, read more in the search for the truth. Read even opposing viewpoints. Don't let the box with deceptive pictures (television) and its comedian 'journalist' be your only source for news and critical information. Strive to achieve critical thinking and subject all liberal issues and arguments for or against the three questions of reason Thomas Sowell spoke of, *"1) compared to what? 2) at what cost? and 3) what hard evidence do you have?"*

Never be afraid of asking the question, Why? Never shy away from debate because debate is the foundation of truth. Opposition or difference in thought from the progressive status quo is now demonized, called hate speech. The actual hate speech is no speech. True hate is going along to get along. Question everything and settle for nothing. Never be afraid to ask questions in your pursuit of the truth because that, my son, is how I raised you, to stand above the crowd, not in the crowd.

It will be all the more important to be armed with the information needed and the critical thinking skills to fight the lies, historical distortions, and propaganda. While there will be numerous issues you will face, all could not be explained in the confines of these essays. Therefore, I penned the first essay as the foundation or standard to which you can thoughtfully examine other issues not listed within the bounds of this book.

In this modern era of liberalism, progressivism, and socialism, all will pull on your emotions and your desire to want fairness, with the goal of supplanting your freedom for their subjective reality. Remember, son, their subjective personal versions of reality are not equivalent to objective truth. Further, such truth can and will sustain itself despite the pressure of emotional debate or the socialist mantra that debate is somehow settled in the hope of squelching the truth.

I know today's society has an intense desire to achieve fame. I need you to understand that myopic approach to life comes at the cost of truth and actual accomplishments. To be a man's son is to accomplish a goal, not to merely be famous. Strive for tangible achievements, and the rest will work itself out.

"Don't try to be a great man, just be a man and let history make its own judgment." ~ Zefram Cochrane (Star Trek)

References

Introduction

[1] Edmund Burke, Thoughts on the Cause of the Present Discontents 82-83 (1770) in: Select Works of Edmund Burke, vol. 1, p. 146 (Liberty Fund ed. 1999).

[2] Thomas Jefferson to Richard Price, 1789. ME 7:253

Chapter 1

[3] Friedrich Hayek, "The Fatal Conceit: The Errors of Socialism", University of Chicago Press, 1988, p.63

[4] Adam Smith, "Wealth of Nations", vol. I, p. 325 (Book II, Chap. III).

[5] Ludwig von Mises, "Liberalism: A Socio-Economic Exposition", Foundation for Economic Education, 1985, p.20

[6] Ludwig von Mises, "Liberalism: A Socio-Economic Exposition", Foundation for Economic Education, 1985, p.20

[7] MD Tanner, "The work-versus-welfare trade-off.", The Cato Institute , 2013,

[8] Larry Schweikart & Michael Allen, "A Patriot's History of the United States: From Columbus's Great Discovery to America's Age of Entitlement", Sentinel, 2014

[9] Data obtained from Maine Department of Health and Human Services

[10] Mary Mayhew, "Commentary: Common sense welfare reforms are taking place in Maine", Portland Press Herald, May 17, 2015,

[11] Fredick Hayek, "The Road to Serfdom", University of Chicago Press, 1944, p153

[12] Milton Friedman, "Why Government Is the Problem", Hoover Institution Press, 1993,

[13] Friedrich Hayek, "The Fatal Conceit: The Errors of Socialism", University of Chicago Press, 1988, p.63

[14] Friedrich Hayek, "The Fatal Conceit: The Errors of Socialism", University of Chicago Press, 1988, p.32

[15] US Census Bureau, "American Community Survey", US Census Bureau, 2010-2014

[16] Stephen Crawford, "The Slave Family: A View from the Slave Narratives", University of Chicago Press, January 1992

[17] Tuskegee Institute, "Lynchings: By State and Race, 1882-1968", Tuskegee Institute

[18] Gunnar Myrdal, "An American Dilemma: The Negro Problem and Modern Democracy", Transaction Publishers, 1944

[19] Gunnar Myrdal, "An American Dilemma: The Negro Problem and Modern Democracy", Transaction Publishers, 1944

[20] John Rosemond, "Is You Child Getting Enough Vitamin N?", Prager University, 2016

[21] John Rosemond, "Is You Child Getting Enough Vitamin N?", Prager University, 2016

[22] Nicole Villalpando, "Physician tells parents, 'You're doing it wrong", Austin American Statesman, January 7, 2017

[23] Todd Starnes, "Shocking! School makes kids take personal responsibility!", Fox News, August 18, 2016

[24] Newsner, " School wants parents to take responsibility - now their poster is spreading like wildfire online:, Newsner, January 18, 2017

[25] Emily Saul, "Brooklyn DA vows to protect illegal immigrants charged with small crimes" New York Post, April 26, 2017

[26] Benjamin Wittes , "What Ben Franklin Really Said", LawFare, July 15, 2011

[27] Benjamin Wittes , "What Ben Franklin Really Said", LawFare, July 15, 2011

[28] Benjamin Wittes , "What Ben Franklin Really Said", LawFare, July 15, 2011

[29] Eugene Volokh, "Shouting fire in a crowded theater", Washington Post, May 11, 2015

[30] Eugene Volokh, "Shouting fire in a crowded theater", Washington Post, May 11, 2015

[31] Milton Friedman, "Free to Choose: A Personal Statement", Mariner Books; 1980, p.29

[32] Alexis de Tocqueville, "Discours prononcé à l'assemblée constituante dans la discussion de projet de constitution (12 Septembre 1848) sur la

question du droit au travail," Oeuvres complètes d'Alexis de Tocqueville, vol. 9 (Paris: Michel Lévy Frères, 1866), p. 546.

[33] Democracy Now, "Vermont's Bernie Sanders Becomes First Socialist Elected to U.S. Senate", November 08, 2006

[34] Jennifer Smith, "Fewer people across the Western world think democracy is 'essential': Less than half of Americans under 50 think they need the right to vote", Daily Mail, November 30, 2016

[35] YouGov survey, January 25 - 27, 2016, ± 4.4% (adjusted for weighting)/ Millennials have a higher opinion of socialism than of capitalism, By Catherine Rampell, Washington Post, February 5, 2016

[36] Emily Ekins, "Why So Many Millennials Are Socialists" , Cata Institute, February 15, 2016

[37] "Millennials Don't Know What "Socialism" Means", Reason-Rupe National Poll, July 16, 2014

[38] Kevin D. Williamson, "The Politically Incorrect Guide to Socialism", Regnery Publishing, 2011

[39] Bulletin of International News, "Herr Hitler's Speech of February 24," Royal Institute of International Affairs, vol. 18, March 8, 1941, p. 269.

[40] Kevin D. Williamson, "The Politically Incorrect Guide to Socialism", Regnery Publishing, 2011, pp.180

[41] W. H. Chamberlin, "Collectivism: A False Utopia", New York: Macmillan, 1937, pp. 202–203.

[42] Milton Friedman, "Capitalism and Freedom", University of Chicago Press, 2002, p.10

[43] Kyle Smith, "Margaret Thatcher Exposed the Infantile Illusions of Socialism", Forbes, April 10, 2013

[44] Ludwig von Mises, "Liberalism: A Socio-Economic Exposition", Foundation for Economic Education, 1985

[45] Ludwig von Mises, "Liberalism: A Socio-Economic Exposition", Foundation for Economic Education, 1985

[46] Milton Friedman, "Free to Choose: A Personal Statement", Mariner Books; 1980,

[47] "Letters from an Inhabitant of Geneva to his Contemporaries," in Henri Saint-Simon (1760–1825): Selected Writings on Science, Industry and Social Organization, trans. and ed. Keith Taylor (New York: Holmes and Meier, 1975), p. 78,

[48] Milton Friedman, "Free to Choose: A Personal Statement", Mariner Books; 1980, p.24

[49] Ludwig von Mises, "Liberalism: A Socio-Economic Exposition", Foundation for Economic Education, 1985, p.67

[50] Democratic Socialists of America Website, http://www.dsausa.org/

[51] Scott Shackford, "Chicago Mayor Threatens Teens' Diplomas Unless They Participate in Approved Post-School Education", Reason, April 5, 2017

[52] Scott Shackford, "Chicago Mayor Threatens Teens' Diplomas Unless They Participate in Approved Post-School Education", Reason, April 5, 2017

[53] Thomas Sowell , "The 'Equality' Racket", Jewish World Review, January 6, 2015

[54] Ludwig von Mises, "Liberalism: A Socio-Economic Exposition", Foundation for Economic Education, 1985

[55] Marian Tupy, " Venezuela Reminds Us That Socialism Frequently Leads to Dictatorship", Reason Blog, April 4, 2017.

[56] Nicholas Casey, "Dying Infants and No Medicine: Inside Venezuela's Failing Hospitals", New York Times, May 15, 2016

[57] Nicholas Casey, "Dying Infants and No Medicine: Inside Venezuela's Failing Hospitals", New York Times, May 15, 2016

[58] Nicholas Casey and Patricia Torres, "Venezuela Drifts Into New Territory: Hunger, Blackouts and Government Shutdown", New York Times, May 28, 2016,

[59] Editorial Board, "Prepare for the worst: Venezuela is heading toward complete disaster", Washington Post, February 11, 2016,

[60] Staff Wrier, "SERIOUS! There are 77 oil plants paralyzed in Venezuela: the warning of a PDVSA worker", El Nacional, March 24, 2017

[61] Frances Martel, "Venezuela, Home to World's Largest Oil Reserves, Runs Out of Gasoline", Breitbart News, March 24th 2017

[62] Frances Martel, "Venezuela, Home to World's Largest Oil Reserves, Runs Out of Gasoline", Breitbart News, March 24th 2017

[63] Kiraz Janicke, "Joseph Stiglitz, in Caracas, Praises Venezuela's Economic Policies", Venezuelanalysis.com, October 11, 2007,

[64] The Dally Current Staff, "Sean Penn Praises Chavez, Calls George Washington a 'Loser", The Dally Current, March 11, 2013

[65] Editorial Board, "Prepare for the worst: Venezuela is heading toward complete disaster", Washington Post, February 11, 2016,

[66] Nicholas Casey and Patricia Torres, "Venezuela Drifts Into New Territory: Hunger, Blackouts and Government Shutdown", New York Times, May 28, 2016,

[67] Marian Tupy, " Venezuela Reminds Us That Socialism Frequently Leads to Dictatorship", Reason Blog, April 4, 2017

[68] Ralph R. Reiland, "How Mugabe is Destroying The Zimbabwean Economy", Capitalism Magazine, Aug 17, 2007,

[69] Richard Washington, "Venezuela calls for mandatory labor in farm sector", CNBC, July 29, 2016,

[70] Pedro Pablo Carreño, "Sundde apply sanctions to bakeries that have tails", El Tiempo, August 18, 2016,

[71] Nicholas Casey And Patricia Torres, "Venezuela Muzzles Legislature, Moving Closer to One-Man Rule", The New York Times, MARCH 30, 2017 / Marian Tupy, " Venezuela Reminds Us That Socialism Frequently Leads to Dictatorship", Reason Blog, April 4, 2017

[72] Donahue Show, "Milton Friedman on Donahue", 1979

[73] Donahue Show, "Milton Friedman on Donahue", 1979

[74] Donahue Show, "Milton Friedman on Donahue", 1979

Chapter 2

[75] Gregory Parker, "Freedom and Democratic Socialism", Conservative Essays for the Modern Era, 2017

[76] Richard Parker, "Five Theses on Identity Politics", Harvard Journal of Law & Public Policy, Vol 29 (1), p.55

[77] Mark Horowitz, William Yaworsky, Kenneth Kickham, "Whither the Blank Slate? A Report on the Reception of Evolutionary Biological Ideas among Sociological Theorists", Sociological Spectrum 34(6), November 2014

[78] John Tierney, "The Real War on Science; The Left has done far more than the Right to set back progress", City Journal, Autumn 2016

[79] Laura Parson, "Are STEM Syllabi Gendered? A Feminist Critical Discourse Analysis", The Qualitative Report, 21(1), p.111.

[80] Laura Parson, "Are STEM Syllabi Gendered? A Feminist Critical Discourse Analysis", The Qualitative Report, 21(1), p.111.

[81] Laura Parson, "Are STEM Syllabi Gendered? A Feminist Critical Discourse Analysis", The Qualitative Report, 21(1), p.111.

82 Chris Enloe, "Fake academic paper published in liberal journal hilariously exposes the absurdity of gender studies", The Blaze, May 21, 2017

83 Peter Boghossian, ED.D & James Lindsay, PH.D, "The Conceptual Penis As A Social Construct: A Sokal-Style Hoax On Gender Studies", The Skeptic, May 19, 2017

84 Peter Boghossian, ED.D & James Lindsay, PH.D, "The Conceptual Penis As A Social Construct: A Sokal-Style Hoax On Gender Studies", The Skeptic, May 19, 2017

85 Amanda Prestigiacomo, "College Students Claim Objective 'Truth' Is A Racist 'Myth'", The Dailywire, April 19, 2017

86 Jim Nelson Black, "When Nations Die", Tyndale House Publishing, 1994, p.6

87 Ray Williams, "Anti-Intellectualism and the "Dumbing Down" of America", Psychology Today, July 7, 2014

88 Ray Williams, "Anti-Intellectualism and the "Dumbing Down" of America", Psychology Today, July 7, 2014

89 Uhls, Y.T., & Greenfield, P.M.., "The Rise of Fame: An Historical Content Analysis.", Cyberpsychology: Journal of Psychosocial Research on Cyberspace, 5(1), article 1, 2011

90 Ray Williams, "Anti-Intellectualism and the "Dumbing Down" of America", Psychology Today, July 7, 2014

91 Ray Williams, "Anti-Intellectualism and the "Dumbing Down" of America", Psychology Today, July 7, 2014

92 Yezmin Villarreal, " Judge Grants Petition for Portland Person to Become 'Agender'", The Advocate, March 27, 2017

93 By Jillian Kay Melchior, " Judge OK's Petition for America's First 'Genderless' Person", Heat Street.com, March 25, 2017

94 Jill Stark, "Call yourself a woman? Feminists take on transgender community in bitter debate", The Sydney Morning Herald, November 22 2015

95 Cleis Abeni, "Feminist Germaine Greer Goes on Anti-Trans Rant Over Caitlyn Jenner", Advocate, October 26 2015

96 Marie Solis, " How the Women's March's "genital-based" feminism isolated the transgender community", MicDaily, January 23, 2017

97 Marie Solis, " How the Women's March's "genital-based" feminism isolated the transgender community", MicDaily, January 23, 2017

[98] Laurie Frankel, "From He to She in First Grade" New York Times, September 16, 2016

[99] Warner Todd Huston, "ACLU Leader Quits, Urges Transgender Compromise, After Men Enter Daughters' Restroom", Breitbart News June 2, 2016

[100] Warner Todd Huston, "ACLU Leader Quits, Urges Transgender Compromise, After Men Enter Daughters' Restroom", Breitbart News June 2, 2016

[101] Kristen Quintrall Lavin, "A Man In The Women's Restroom At Disneyland", The Get Real Mom Blog, March 13, 2017

[102] Klaudia Van Emmerik, " Concerns over transgender client at Okanagan shelter", Global News, March 9, 2017

[103] Chloe Valdary, "Don't Judge Blacks Differently", Video by Prager University

[104] Rick Ross, "Ten warning signs of a potentially unsafe group/leader", The Cult Education Institute

[105] Christine Hauser, "Texas Mayor Announces That She Is Transgender", The New York Times, Feburary 1, 2017

[106] Matt Moore, "Why Can't Gay Activists Tolerate People Who Are No Longer Practicing Homosexuals?", The Christian Post, August 12, 2014

[107] Sadie Gennis, "Jerry Seinfeld Thinks Political Correctness Is Killing Comedy", TV Guild Todays News, June 8, 2015

[108] Liam Mathews, "John Cleese Thinks Political Correctness Is Killing Comedy", TV Guild Todays News, February 1, 2016

[109] Alexander Bisley, "Anthony Bourdain on Sichuan Peppers, Sex, Eating Dogs, and Political Correctness", Interview – Reason.com, December 29, 2016

[110] Matt Walsh, "Wake Up, Christians. There Is No Place For You In The Democrat Party", The Blaze, July 28, 2016

[111] "The Diagnostic and Statistical Manual of Mental Disorders (DSM-V)", American Psychiatric Association, May 18, 2013

[112] Lucy Nicholson, "Obama says transgender bathroom directive based on law", Reuters, September 30, 2014

[113] Ben Rohrbach, "Transgender track athlete makes history as controversy swirls around her", USA Today High School Sports, June 2, 2016

[114] Abbott Koloff, " Boy Scouts to pay $18,000, apologize to 9-year-old transgender boy thrown out of pack", North Jersey Record, March 2, 2017

[115] Courtney Crowder, "Iowa's First Transgender High School Athlete Found His Truth On The Track", USA Today High School Sports, August 5, 2016

[116] Cecilia Dhejne, Paul Lichtenstein, Marcus Boman, Anna L. V. Johansson, Niklas Långström, Mikael Landén , "Long-term Follow Up of Transsexual Persons Undergoing Sex Reassignment Surgery: Cohort Study in Sweden", PLOS One, February 22, 2011

[117] Dr Joseph Berger, "Comments to House of Commons Standing Committee on Justice and Human Right, 2013

[118] Michelle A. Cretella, M.D., Quentin Van Meter, M.D., Paul McHugh, M.D., "Gender Ideology Harms Children", American College of Pediatricians, January 2017

[119] Kay Dibben, " Minority of children with gender issues diagnosed with gender dysphoria, psychiatrist says ", The Courier-Mail April 8, 2017

[120] Dr. Susan Berry, "Transgender Activist: Preference for Kids Single-Sex Shower Rooms is 'Prejudiced", Breitbart News, Febuary 27, 2017

[121] Dr. Susan Berry, "Transgender Activist: Preference for Kids Single-Sex Shower Rooms is 'Prejudiced", Breitbart News, Febuary 27, 2017

[122] Walt Heyer, "I Used to Be Transgender. Here's My Take on Kids Who Think They Are Transgender.", Thr Daily Signal, February 16, 2016

[123] Walt Heyer, "50 Years of Sex Changes, Mental Disorders, and Too Many Suicides", The Witherspoon Institute, February 2, 2016

[124] Neil W. Mccabe, "Gohmert: The Only Science Behind Transgender Agenda Is Political Science", Capitol Hill, June 10, 2016

[125] Margaret A. Hagen, "Transgenderism Has No Basis in Science or Law", The Witherspoon Institute, January 2016

[126] Andrew R. Flores, Taylor N.T. Brown, Andrew S. Park, " Public Support for Transgender Rights: A Twenty-three Country Survey", The Williams Institute, December 2016

[127] Paul McHugh, "Transgender A Pathogenic Meme", The Witherspoon Institute, June, 2015

[128] Dr Joseph Berger, "Comments to House of Commons Standing Committee on Justice and Human Right, 2013

[129] Paul Joseph Watson, "21-Year-Old Woman Lives As Baby", The Witherspoon Institute, August 1, 2016

[130] Jim Nelson Black, "When Nations Die", Tyndale House Publishing, 1994, p.xvii

[131] Ashifa Kassam, "A Transgender Man And Gay Partner Wanted To Have Children And 'Chestfeed' Babies", The Guardian, June 20, 2016

[132] Amanda Prestigiacomo, "21-Year-Old Woman Lives As 'Adult Baby' With Boyfriend As 'Daddy'", The Daily Wire, August 2, 2016

[133] Associated Press, "Convicted killer receives first state-funded sex-reassignment surgery in California prison", Associated Press, January 7, 2016

[134] Associated Press, "Convicted killer receives first state-funded sex-reassignment surgery in California prison", Associated Press, January 7, 2016

[135] April Horning, " California Boasts Country's First Taxpayer-Funded Gender Change…Until The Results End In Disaster", Conservative Daily Post, March 23, 2017

[136] Ruth Padawer, "When Women Become Men at Wellesley", The New York Times, October 15, 2014

[137] Christina Coleman, "GlobalGrind History Lesson: The Real Reason It's Just Not OK To Wear Blackface (LIST)", Globalgrind, nd.

[138] Christina Coleman, "GlobalGrind History Lesson: The Real Reason It's Just Not OK To Wear Blackface (LIST)", Globalgrind, nd.

[139] Edwin L. Marin, "Everybody Sing", USA, Metro-Goldwyn-Mayer (MGM), 1938

[140] "Jason Aldean wore blackface, dressed as Lil Wayne for Halloween, his rep confirms", Associated Press, November 10, 2015

[141] Telepictures Productions, The Real, Warner Bros. Domestic Television Distribution, 2015

[142] Sincere Kirabo, "Rachel Dolezal's Book Deal Underscores the Myth of Transracial Identity", The Humanist, April 20, 2016

[143] Sincere Kirabo, "The Myth of Transracial Identity", The Humanist, April 18, 2016

[144] Courtney Kirchoff, "Caught Black Lives Matter Activist Shaun King is Actually White", Louder with Crowder, August 19, 2015

[145] Feliks Garcia, "The rise and fall of Shaun King, former Black Lives Matter darling", Complex.com, January 29, 2016

[146] JT30, "An Open Letter From Former Directors of Justice Together", November 13, 2015

[147] Feliks Garcia, "The rise and fall of Shaun King, former Black Lives Matter darling", Complex.com, January 29, 2016

[148] Joshua Marcus, "This Is Why I No Longer Identify As White", Huffington Post, February 22, 2017

[149] Steven W. Thrasher, "Afrofuturism: reimagining science and the future from a black perspective", The Guardian, December 7, 2015

[150] Sincere Kirabo, "Rachel Dolezal's Book Deal Underscores the Myth of Transracial Identity", The Humanist, April 20, 2016

[151] Juliana Menasce Horowitz and Gretchen Livingston, "How Americans view the Black Lives Matter movement", Pew Research Center, July 8, 2016

[152] Rudy Takala , "Hacked: Dems warned candidates against saying 'all lives matter", The Washington Examiner, August 31, 2016

[153] Roland C. Warren, "Black Lives Matter's real agenda", The Washington Times, July 28, 2016

[154] Black Lives Matter Web Site, www.blacklivesmatter.com, August 1, 2016

[155] Gregory Parker, "Freedom and Democratic Socialism", Conservative Essays for the Modern Era, 2017

[156] See this essay section on 'Transracial the new blackface' - Gregory Parker, "Conservative Essays for the Modern Era", 2017

[157] Derryck Green, "The 'Black Lives Matter' Slogan Ignores Self-Destructive Behavior", Project 21, n.d.

[158] Jacob Steele, "If Black Lives Matter Why Do Blacks Treat Themselves And Each Other So Badly", Patriot Update, August 24, 2015

[159] Dave Urbanski, "Black Lives Matter leader: Police officers 'evolved' from 'slave catchers", The Blaze, March 22, 2017

[160] Dave Urbanski, "Black Lives Matter leader: Police officers 'evolved' from 'slave catchers", The Blaze, March 22, 2017

[161] OrthodoxyToday Staff Writer, "How Planned Parenthood Duped America", OrthodoxyToday.org, 2001

[162] Black Lives Matter Web Site, www.blacklivesmatter.com, August 1, 2016

[163] Stephen Crawford, "The Slave Family: A View from the Slave Narratives", University of Chicago Press, January 1992

[164] "Black Lives Matter's real agenda", Roland C. Warren, The Washington Times, July 28, 2016

[165] Black Lives Matter Web Site, www.blacklivesmatter.com, August 1, 2016

[166] Black Lives Matter Web Site, www.blacklivesmatter.com, August 1, 2016

[167] Black Lives Matter Web Site, www.blacklivesmatter.com, August 1, 2016

[168] Guy Adams, "The children of privilege who loathe the system that gave them every advantage: The truth about the (white) Black Lives Matter protesters who closed London City airport... and why you'll want to protest against THEM", The Daily Mail, September 16, 2016,

[169] Walter Williams, "The Ugly Racism of Karl Marx", The Daily Signal, May 10, 2017 / Nathaniel Weyl, "Karl Marx, racist", Arlington House; First Edition, 1979

[170] Jeremy Beaman, "Cal State LA offers segregated housing for black students", The College Fix, September 6, 2016

[171] Jeremy Beaman, "Cal State LA offers segregated housing for black students", The College Fix, September 6, 2016

[172] Amanda Prestigiacomo, " Students Protesting Racism Segregate Themselves: 'White Students To The Front!'", The Dailywire, April 10, 2017

[173] Paul Meara, "Here's Why Black Harvard Students Are Holding Their Own Graduation Ceremony", BET Online, May 7, 2017

[174] Nikole Hannah-Jones, "Segregation Now", The Atlantic, May 2014

[175] Rucker C. Johnson, "Long-Run Impacts Of School Desegregation & School Quality On Adult Attainments", National Bureau Of Economic Research, January 2011

[176] Rucker C. Johnson, "Long-Run Impacts Of School Desegregation & School Quality On Adult Attainments", National Bureau Of Economic Research, January 2011

[177] Chase Stephens, "Black Lives Matter Just Banned White People", The Dailywire, April 3, 2017

[178] Aeman Ansari , "Ethnic Minorities Deserve Safe Spaces Without White People", Huffington Post, March 18, 2015

Chapter 3
[179] Ludwig Von Mises, "The Anti-capitalistic Mentality", Liberty Fund, 2006, p.1065

[180] Ayn Rand, "Capitalism: The Unknown Ideal", Signet; Reissue edition, 1986, p10

[181] Lawrence W. Reed, "7 Fallacies of Economics", Northwood Institute, 1981

[182] Gregory Parker, "Freedom and Democratic Socialism", "Conservative Essays for the Modern Era", 2017

[183] Gregory Parker, "Freedom and Democratic Socialism", "Conservative Essays for the Modern Era", 2017

[184] Ayn Rand, "Capitalism: The Unknown Ideal", Signet; Reissue edition, 1986, p10

[185] Kevin D. Williamson, "The Politically Incorrect Guide to Socialism", Regnery Publishing, 2011

[186] Ann Rand

[187] Ludwig von Mises, "Liberalism: A Socio-Economic Exposition", Foundation for Economic Education, 1985, p.67

[188] Milton Friedman, "Free to Choose: A Personal Statement", Mariner Books; 1980, p.24

[189] Kevin D. Williamson, "The Politically Incorrect Guide to Socialism", Regnery Publishing, 2011, p.9

[190] Thomas Sewell, "Has Economics Failed", The National Review, November 2, 2016 / Henry Hazlitt, "The Wisdom of Henry Hazlitt", Irvington-on-Hudson, NY: The Foundation for Economic Education, 1993, p. 329.

[191] Milton Friedman, "Capitalism and Freedom", University of Chicago Press, 2002, p.10

[192] Kevin D. Williamson, "The Politically Incorrect Guide to Socialism", Regnery Publishing, 2011, p.12

[193] Staff Wrier, "SERIOUS! There are 77 oil plants paralyzed in Venezuela: the warning of a PDVSA worker", El Nacional, March 24, 2017

[194] Frances Martel, "Venezuela, Home to World's Largest Oil Reserves, Runs Out of Gasoline", Breitbart News, March 24th 2017

[195] Frances Martel, "Venezuela, Home to World's Largest Oil Reserves, Runs Out of Gasoline", Breitbart News, March 24th 2017

[196] Ralph R. Reiland, "How Mugabe is Destroying The Zimbabwean Economy", Capitalism Magazine, August 17, 2007,

[197] Eric Boehm, " Venezuela Arrests Bakers for Making Rolls, Claims They Were Waging 'Economic War' Against Country:, Reason Blog, March 22, 2017

[198] Jim Wyss, " Venezuela has a bread shortage. The government has decided bakers are the problem." The Miami Herald, March 16, 2017

[199] Terry Jones, "The Bitter Lesson From Seattle's Minimum Wage Hike", Investors Business Daily, August 10, 2016

[200] Andrew Kuuleme, "De Blasio Raises His Rents While Pushing Rent-Control Policy", The Washington Free Beacon, April 17, 2017

[201] Thomas Sowell , "Economic Facts and Fallacies", Basic books, 2008, p.219

[202] Thomas Sowell , "Economic Facts and Fallacies", Basic books, 2008, p.3

[203] Ludwig Von Mises, "The Anti-capitalistic Mentality", Liberty Fund Publishing, 2006, p.1044

[204] Terry Miller & Anthony B. Kim, "Economic Freedom in America", The Heritage Foundation, 2016

[205] Alana Marie Burke , "Barack Obama Solyndra Scandal: 8 Facts About Green Energy Company Controversy", Newsmax, January 29, 2015

[206] Joe Stephens & Carol D. Leonnig, "Solyndra: Politics infused Obama energy programs", The Washington Post, December 25, 2011

[207] Walter Williams, "The Pursuit of Happiness", Ideas On Liberty, January 2000

[208] Thomas Sowell, "Dismantling America: and other controversial essays", Basic Books, Kindle Edition p. 151

[209] Wesley Gant, "Greed is not Good But Self-interest is", Values & Capitalism, 3013

[210] Dennis Prager, "Socialism Makes People Selfish", Prager University, 2016

[211] Dennis Prager, "Socialism Makes People Selfish", Prager University, 2016

[212] Helena Andrews-Dyer , "Bernie Sanders buys a $575,000 vacation home and the Internet cries hypocrisy", The Washington Post, August 10

[213] US Census Bureau, "Quarterly Residential Vacancies and Homeownership, October 27, 2016

[214] Emily Zanotti, " Marxist Vegan Restaurant Closes After Customers No Longer Willing to Wait 40 Minutes for a Sandwich", Heatstreet, December 8, 2016

[215] Emily Zanotti, " Marxist Vegan Restaurant Closes After Customers No Longer Willing to Wait 40 Minutes for a Sandwich", Heatstreet, December 8, 2016

[216] Houman Salem, "Leaving for Las Vegas: California's minimum wage law leaves businesses no choice", Las Angels Times, January 2, 2017

[217] BBC News, "Venezuela minimum wage to rise by 50% 'to combat inflation", January 9, 2017

218 Arthur Brooks, "Five myths about free enterprise", The Washington Post, July 13, 2012

219 Pew Research Center, "Pew Research Center For The People & The Press 2012 Values Survey", April 4-15, 2012

220 Arthur Brooks, "Five myths about free enterprise", The Washington Post, July 13, 2012

221 Ludwig Von, Mises "Anti Capitalist Mentality", Liberty Fund Publishing, 2006, p308 (Kindle Version)

222 Deirdre N. Mccloskey, "Growth, Not Forced Equality, Saves the Poor", The New York Times, December 23, 2016

223 Milton Friedman, "Lecture to Standford University", 1978

224 Friedrich Hayek, "The Road to Serfdom", University of Chicago Press., 2007 Kindle Edition, p.3281

225 Bernadette D. Proctor, Jessica L. Semega, Melissa A. Kollar, "Income and Poverty in the United States: 2015, U.S. Census Bureau, Report Number: P60-256- September 13, 2016

226 Robert Rector and Rachel Sheffield," Air Conditioning, Cable TV, and an Xbox: What Is Poverty in the United States Today?", The Heritage Foundation, July 18, 2011

227 Bourguignon, François and Christian Morrisson, "Inequality Among World Citizens: 1820-1992 ." American Economic Review, 2002, 92(4): 727-744 / Max Roser and Esteban Ortiz-Ospina, "Global Extreme Poverty", Published online at OurWorldInData.org, 2017

228 Max Roser and Esteban Ortiz-Ospina, "Global Extreme Poverty", Published online at OurWorldInData.org, 2017

229 World Bank PovcalNet data post 2017

230 World Bank PovcalNet data post 2017

231 World Bank PovcalNet data post 2017

232 World Bank PovcalNet data post 2017

233 Marian Tupy, " Venezuela Reminds Us That Socialism Frequently Leads to Dictatorship", Reason Blog, April 4, 2017.

234 Marian Tupy, " Venezuela Reminds Us That Socialism Frequently Leads to Dictatorship", Reason Blog, April 4, 2017

235 James Pethokoukis, " North Korea vs. South Korea, a natural economic experiment", American Enterprise Institute, December, 20, 2011

236 Frances Martel, " North Korea Warns Starving Population: Famine Is Coming", Breitbart News, March 30, 2016

[237] Frances Martel, " North Korea Warns Starving Population: Famine Is Coming", Breitbart News, March 30, 2016

[238] The Heritage Foundation, "2017 Index of Economic Freedom - South Korea", 2017

[239] Terry Miller & Anthony B. Kim, "2016 Index of Economic Freedom", The Heritage Foundation, 2016, pp.VII

[240] Gregory Parker, "Freedom and Democratic Socialism", "Conservative Essays for the Modern Era", 2017

Chapter 4

[241] The Second Amendment to the U.S. Constitution, 1776

[242] David Barton, "the Second Amendment", WallBuilder Press; 1st edition, 2000

[243] Gregory Parker, "Freedom and Democratic Socialism", Conservative Essays for the Modern Era, 2017,

[244] Thomas Jefferson, Memoir, Correspondence, and Miscellanies, Thomas Jefferson Randolph, editor (Boston: Gray and Bowen, 1830), Vol. IV, p. 373, to Judge William Johnson on June 12, 1823.

[245] James Wilson, The Works of the Honorable James Wilson, Bird Wilson, editor (Philadelphia: Bronson and Chauncey, 1804), Vol. I, p. 14, from "Lectures on Law Delivered in the College of Philadelphia; Introductory Lecture: Of the Study of the Law in the United States.

[246] Alexander Hamilton, "The Farmer Refuted: Or, A More Impartial partial and Comprehensive View of the Dispute Between Great Britain and the Colonies", New York: James Rivington, 1775, p. 6.

[247] William Blackstone, "Commentaries on the Laws", Philadelphia: phia: Robert Bell, 1771, Vol. I, pp. 143-144.

[248] Zephaniah Swift, "A System of the Laws of the State of Connecticut cut", Windham: John Byrne, 1796, Vol. II, p 302; see also Vol. II, p. 2.

[249] Blackstone's Commentaries: With Notes and Reference, St. George Tucker, editor (Philadelphia: William Young Birch, and Abraham Small, 1803), Vol. I, p. 300.

[250] Cockrum v. State, 24 Tex. 394, at 401-402 (1859)]

[251] Larry Schweikart & Michael Patrick Allen, "The Patriot History A Patriot's History of the United States: From Columbus's Great Discovery to America's Age of Entitlement, Revised Edition", Sentinel; 10th Revised ed. edition, 2014, p324, kindle version

[252] Samuel Adams, Writings, Vol. III, p. 251, to James Warren on January 7, 1776.

[253] Debates ... of the Convention of Virginia, p. 302, George Mason on June 16, 1788; see also Elliot's Debates, Vol. III, p. 425 (Elliot's incorrectly lists the date as June 14; it is properly June 16).

[254] U.S. v. Emerson, 5th court of Appeals decision, November 2, 2001, No. 99-10331

[255] U.S. v. Emerson, 5th court of Appeals decision, November 2, 2001, No. 99-10331

[256] District of Columbia v. Heller, 554 U.S. 570 (2008).

[257] Jeffrey M. Jones, "Americans in Agreement With Supreme Court on Gun Rights", Gallup, June 26, 2008

[258] The First Amendment to the U.S. Constitution, 1776

[259] Stephen P. Holbrook, "That Every Man Be Armed: Evolution of a Constitutional Right", University of New Mexico Press; Updated Edition, 2013

[260] Cesare Beccaria, "An Essay on Crimes & Punishments", New York: Stephen Gould, 1809, p. 124-25. (translated from the Italian with a commentary, attributed to M. de Voltaire, translated from the French)

[261] Richard Pérez-Peña, "Gun Control Explained", The New York Times, October 7, 2015

[262] Justin Curmi, "A Revision on the Bill of Rights, Part III", The Huffington Post, April 26, 2017

[263] Dave Urbanski, "Even a criminal has rights': Dead robbery suspect's parents angry that store worker shot their son", The Blaze, November 4, 2016

[264] Dave Urbanski, "Even a criminal has rights': Dead robbery suspect's parents angry that store worker shot their son", The Blaze, November 4, 2016

[265] Nevada Senate bill SB-254, Filed March 9 2017

[266] Art Swift, "Personal Safety Top Reason Americans Own Guns Today", Gallup, October 28, 2013

[267] Guy Smith, "Gun Facts Version 7.0", 2015, pp.62

[268] Guy Smith, "Gun Facts Version 7.0", 2015, pp.62

[269] Lacey Wallace, "Research shows gun purchases go up after mass shootings", Raw Story Online, December 8, 2015

[270] John R. Lott, "The War on Guns: Arming Yourself Against Gun Control Lies", Regnery Publishing, 2016

[271] John R. Lott, "Concealed Carry Permit Holders Across the United States:, Crime Prevention Research Center, 2016

[272] "Pink Pistols LGBT gun club triples in size after Orlando",June 28, 2016, The Guardian.com

[273] "Pink Pistols LGBT gun club triples in size after Orlando",June 28, 2016, The Guardian.com

[274] Alex Newman, "Amid Terror in Paris, Gun Control Leaves French Defenseless", The New American, January 9, 2015

[275] Romina McGuinness, "French police demand right to carry guns as nation faces Islamic threat", Daily Express, Aug 9, 2016

[276] Romina McGuinness, "French police demand right to carry guns as nation faces Islamic threat", Daily Express, Aug 9, 2016

[277] Staff Writer, "Bulletproof vests proposed banned in Sweden", Speisa.com, February 17, 2017

[278] Staff Writer, "Bulletproof vests proposed banned in Sweden", Speisa.com, February 17, 2017

[279] Yanan Wang, " Ex-Calif. State Sen. Leland Yee, gun control champion, heading to prison for weapons trafficking", The Washington Post, February 25, 2016

[280] Yanan Wang, " Ex-Calif. State Sen. Leland Yee, gun control champion, heading to prison for weapons trafficking", The Washington Post, February 25, 2016

[281] "Lena Dunham Calls for Altering of Gun-Toting 'Jason Bourne' Subway Ads", Arlene Washington, July 12, 2016, The Hollywood Reporter

[282] Matt Damon Says 'Jason Bourne' Is Keeping His Guns", Katie Jerkovich, July 21, 2016, The Daily Caller

[283] Malcolm X Speaks, Merit Publishers, 1965

[284] Markus T. Funk, "Gun Control and Economic Discrimination: The Melting-Point Case-in-Point," The Journal of Criminal Law and Criminology, 1995.

[285] Clayton E. Cramer, "The Racist Roots of Gun Control", 1993

[286] David Babat, "The Discriminatory History of Gun Control", University of Rhode Island, 2009

[287] Adam Winkler, " Gunfight: The Battle over the Right to Bear Arms in America", W. W. Norton & Company, 2011

[288] Watson v. Stone, 4So,2d 700, 703 (Fla. 1941)

[289] Assembly Office of Research, "Smoking Gun: The Case For Concealed W eapon Permit Reform", Sacramento, State of California, 1986

[290] John R. Lott, "Concealed Carry Permit Holders Across the United States:, Crime Prevention Research Center, 2016

[291] Kelly Riddell, "Data divulges racial disparity in Chicago's issuance of gun permits", The Washington Times, September 29, 2014

[292] Kelly Riddell, "Data divulges racial disparity in Chicago's issuance of gun permits", The Washington Times, September 29, 2014

[293] Kelly Riddell, "Data divulges racial disparity in Chicago's issuance of gun permits", The Washington Times, September 29, 2014

[294] Mike Lillis, "Democrat's bill targets 'junk' handguns," The Hill, March 4, 2013,

[295] Staff, "From Veep to Lobbyist: Biden Pressures CO Democratic Lawmakers to Pass Gun Control," Colorado Peak Politics, February 15, 2013 / Lott, John R.. The War on Guns: Arming Yourself Against Gun Control Lies (Kindle Locations 3091-3092). Regnery Publishing. Kindle Edition.

[296] Lott, John R.. The War on Guns: Arming Yourself Against Gun Control Lies (Kindle Location 194). Regnery Publishing. Kindle Edition.

[297] Dave Urbanski, "Even a criminal has rights': Dead robbery suspect's parents angry that store worker shot their son", The Blaze, November 4, 2016

[298] Dave Urbanski, "Black Lives Matter leader: Police officers 'evolved' from 'slave catchers", The Blaze, March 22, 2017

[299] Jennifer Abel, "Who has advantage in a gun-free zone?", Middletown Press, December 13, 2008

[300] Pete Kasperowicz, "Democrats push to ban guns at airports, leave people vulnerable to attacks by armed gunmen", Washington Examiner, March 29, 2017

[301] John R. Lott Jr, "A Look at the Facts on Gun-Free Zones", National Review, October 20, 2015.

[302] Patrick Tyrrell, " Mass Shooters Prefer Gun-Free Zones", The Heritage Foundation, Febuary 10, 2016

[303] Patrick Tyrrell, "Mass Shooters Prefer Gun-Free Zones", The Heritage Foundation, Febuary 10, 2016

[304] Erica L. Smith and Alexia Cooper, Ph.D, " Homicide in the U.S. Known to Law Enforcement, 2011", U.S. Department of Justice, December 2013

[305] CDC - Mortality/ Deaths: Final Data for 2014

[306] William J. Krouse, "Gun Control Legislation, Congressional Research Service, Noverber 14, 2013

[307] William J. Krouse, "Gun Control Legislation, Congressional Research Service, Noverber 14, 2013

Chapter 5

[308] Sig Christenson, "Hasan cites a motive for attack", San Antonio Express News, June 4, 2013

[309] Alastair Jamieson and David Taintor, " Draw Muhammad' shooting in Texas: 5 things to know", MSNBC, May 4, 2015

[310] Kristi Eaton & Corinne Lestch & Corky Siemaszko " Oklahoma man beheads woman, stabs 2nd victim during workplace fight day after being fired from job", New York Daily News, September 26, 2014

[311] Justen Charters, " 33 Things We Learned About the Oklahoma Beheading Suspect: What His Hand Signal Means Will Chill You", Independent Journal Review, 2014

[312] Bill Warner, "A Self-Study Course On Political Islam Level 1", Cspi Publishing, Inc., 2011, p.10

[313] Bill Warner, "A Self-Study Course On Political Islam Level 1", Cspi Publishing, Inc., 2011, p.12

[314] Bill Warner, "A Self-Study Course On Political Islam Level 1", Cspi Publishing, Inc., 2011

[315] Richard Butrick, "The Two Faces of Islam", American Thinker, August 31, 2014

[316] Bill Warner, "A Self-Study Course On Political Islam Level 1", Cspi Publishing, Inc., 2011, p. 9

[317] Charles Moore, "It gives Muslims a bad name': British boxer Amir Khan accuses terrorists of perverting his religion and reveals he fears his daughter will be targeted by racists", The Daily Mail, May 24, 2017

[318] Amber Athey, "Twitter Liberals Worry About Muslims' Feelings After Manchester Bombing", The Daily Caller, May 24, 2017

[319] Amber Athey, "Twitter Liberals Worry About Muslims' Feelings After Manchester Bombing", The Daily Caller, May 24, 2017

[320] Sarfaz Manzoor, "Can we drop the term 'moderate Muslim'? It's meaningless", The Guardian News, March 16, 2015

[321] Pew Research Center, "The Future of World Religions: Population Growth Projections, 2010-2050", April 2, 2015

[322] Pew Research Center, "The Future of World Religions: Population Growth Projections, 2010-2050", April 2, 2015

323 Michael Lipka, "Muslims and Islam: Key findings in the U.S. and around the world", Pew Research Center, April 2, 2015
324 Aaron Bandler, "PragerU Video: Where Are The Moderate Muslims?", The Daily Wire, April 28, 2017
325 James Bell, "The World's Muslims: Religion, Politics and Society", Pew Research Center Forum, April 30, 2013
326 Staff reporter, "Hardline Kenya cleric, the face of homegrown radical Islam", Africatime Cameroon, March 11, 2014
327 Roberto Saviano, "The Worldwide War Against Free Speech", Vice, March 5, 2015
328 Jon Stone, "Charlie Hebdo journalists 'provoked' their own slaughter with 'disgusting record', says American Catholic group", The Independent, January 8, 2015
329 Gregory Parker, "Conservative Essays for the Modern Era - Identity Politics: Felling Over Facts" Parker Press, LLC., 2017
330 Kim Willsher, " Fears Paris shooting will affect presidential election as first round looms", The Guardian, April 21, 2017
331 Jack Montgomery, "French Presidential Favourite Macron: Terrorism 'Part of Our Daily Lives for Years to Come' After Paris Shooting", Breitbart News, April 21, 2017
332 Staff Writer, "Germany will become an Islamic State, says Merkel – and adds they'll have to come to terms with it ", JewsNews, May 7, 2017
333 Pamela Geller, "Outraged Muslims to March Against Amazon Over Muslim Prayer Breaks", The Geller Report, April 22, 2017
334 Gregory Parker, Conservative Essays: For the Modern Era", Parker Press, LLC., 2017
335 Center for Security Policy, "U.S. Muslim Brotherhood and Saul Alinsky: A Match Made in America", March 28, 2017
336 Kellan Howell, "Citadel mulls allowing Muslim cadet to wear hijab, first religious uniform exception", The Washington Times, April 15, 2016
337 Nicholas Kurch, "A Muslim Woman is Suing Michigan Police for Violating Her Religious Freedom During a Routine Arrest", Independant Journal Review, 2015
338 Hank Berrien, "Submission: Canada Passes Anti-Islamophobia Bill" , The Daily Wire, March 23, 2017
339 Hank Berrien, "Submission: Canada Passes Anti-Islamophobia Bill" , The Daily Wire, March 23, 2017

[340] Hank Berrien, "Submission: Canada Passes Anti-Islamophobia Bill" , The Daily Wire, March 23, 2017

[341] Religion Foundation v. Concord Community Schools, Case No. 3:15-CV-463 JD, United States District Court Northern District Of Indiana South Bend Division

[342] Gary Warth, "San Diego Unified to fight Islamophobia, bullying", San Diego Union Tribune, April 5, 2017

[343] Ed Barmakian, "Chatham Parents Question Emphasis on Islam in 7th Grade World Cultures and Geography Class", TapInto , Febuary 7, 2017

[344] "Supreme Court Skips Dispute Over Islam Instruction," American United for Separation of Church and State, November 2006

[345] Kimiko de Freytas-Tamura, "Danish Man Who Burned Quran Is Prosecuted for Blasphemy", The New York Times, Febuary 23, 2017

[346] Jamie Schram, Larry Celona and Joe Tacopino, "Muslim newlyweds slaughter co-workers who threw them a baby shower", New York Post, December 3, 2015

[347] Christopher Mele, "Muslim Woman Made Up Hate Crime on Subway, Police Say", The New York Times, December 14, 2016

[348] Derek Hawkins and Fred Barbash, "Louisiana student 'fabricated' story of hijab attack, police say", The Washington Post, November 10, 2016

[349] Andrew O'Riley, "Labor group levels charges of union busting against Muslim rights organization", Fox News, April 21,2017

[350] Nathan Wold, "10 Of The Craziest Ideas Pushed In The Name Of Feminism", List Verse, December 25, 2014

[351] Amanda Prestigiacomo, "Top Ten Batsh*t-Crazy Feminist Fails of 2015", The Daily Wire, December 28, 2015

[352] Nathan Wold, "10 Of The Craziest Ideas Pushed In The Name Of Feminism", List Verse, December 25, 2014

[353] Christopher Dickey, "The Fire That Won't Die Out", NewsWeek, July 21, 2002 / Robert Spencer, "The Politically Incorrect Guide to Islam", Regnery Publishing, 2005, p. 68 Kindle Edition.

[354] Reuters, "Iranian beheads daughter, suspecting she was raped", Daily News, September 9, 2002

[355] Reuters, "Iranian beheads daughter, suspecting she was raped", Daily News, September 9, 2002

[356] Staff Reporter, " Muslim men can rape non-Muslim women to teach them a lesson, claims woman Islamic professor", India News, April 16, 2017

357 Olver JJ Lane, " Cologne Imam: Girls Were Raped Because They Were Half Naked And Wore Perfume", Breitbart News, January 19, 2016
358 Laurie Penny, "This isn't 'feminism'. It's Islamophobia", The Guardian, December 22, 2013
359 Susan Goldberg, "Girl Scout Who Confronted Neo-Nazi Admits Immigrants May Rape Her, Says She'll Get Over It", PJ Media, May 6, 2017
360 Staff Reporter, "Husband has right to beat wife rules court of cassation", Gulf News, March 31, 2002
361 Theresa Corbin, " I'm a feminist and I converted to Islam", CNN, October 14, 2014
362 Jo Dixon, "Feminist Theory and Domestic Violence", Encyclopedia of Criminology and Criminal Justice, 2014, pp 1612-1617
363 Bell Hooks, "Feminism is for Everybody", Pluto Press, 2000, p.62.
364 Staff, "Does Islam encourage violence against women? Read to find out!", Muslim Inc., Accessed 2017
365 Robert Spencer, "The Politically Incorrect Guide to Islam", Regnery Publishing, 2005, p.70. Kindle Edition.
366 Andrew Bushell, "Child Marriage in Afghanistan and Pakistan," America, March 11, 2002,
367 Beth Potier, " Reconciling faith with feminism:, Harvard Gazette, November 7, 2002
368 Robert Spencer and Phyllis Chesler, "Violent Oppression of Women in Islam", Frontpage Magazine, March 11, 2002, p. 12
369 Amir Taheri, The Spirit of Allah: Khomeini and the Islamic Revolution (New York: Adler and Adler), 1986, 90–91.
Spencer, Robert. The Politically Incorrect Guide to Islam (And the Crusades) (The Politically Incorrect Guides) (p. 242). Regnery Publishing. Kindle Edition.
370 Robert Spencer & Phillis Chesler, "The Violent Oppression of Women In Islam", David Horowitz Freedom Center, 2007
371 "Harmful Traditional Practices and Implementation of the Law On Elimination of Violence Against Women in Afghanistan", UNAMA & OHCHR, p.18-21. December 9, 2010.
372 Lisa Beyer, "The Women of Islam," Time, November 25, 2001.
373 Victoria Richards, "Child marriage chart reveals girls can wed at 12 in some parts of the US - as lawmakers battle to raise age to 16", The Independent Daily, March 9, 2016

[374] Jasmine Garsd, " Child brides are a little-known, but very real, problem in America today", PRI's The World, March 17, 2017

[375] World Health Organization, "Female Genital Mutilation (FGM), February 2017

[376] Jason Howerton, "Police Arrest Detroit ER Doctor for Performing Female Genital Mutilations Out of Her Private Office", Independent Journal Review, April 13, 2017 / Robert Snell, " 2nd doctor, wife arrested in genital mutilation case ", The Detroit News, April 21, 2017

[377] Caitlin Yoshiko Kandil, "Training Hopes to Build 'Pipeline' for Muslim Candidates After Trump Election", The Washington Post, April 13, 2017

[378] Alastair Jamieson and Michele Neubert, "Orlando Highlights Islam's Complicated Relationship With Homosexuality", NBC News, July 12, 2016

[379] Alastair Jamieson and Michele Neubert, "Orlando Highlights Islam's Complicated Relationship With Homosexuality", NBC News, July 12, 2016

[380] Robert Spencer, " Tunisian Imam: Homosexuals should be stoned to death", Jihad Watch, May 4, 2016

[381] "Orlando terror attack updates: Obama meets with victims' families in Orlando", NBC News June 16, 2016

[382] Milo Yiannopoulo, "The Left Chose Islam Over Gays. Now 100 People Are Dead Or Maimed In Orlando", Breitbart News, June 12, 2016

[383] Nick Gutteridge, "Fury as watchdog says it's OK to send gay people death threats – but only if you're Muslim", Daily Express UK, December 3, 2016

[384] Thomas Burrows, "Chechnya opens world's first concentration camp for homosexuals since Hitler's in the 1930s where campaigners say gay men are being tortured with electric shocks and beaten to death", Daily Mail, April 10, 2017

www.ingramcontent.com/pod-product-compliance
Lightning Source LLC
Chambersburg PA
CBHW032135020426
42334CB00016B/1175